Butterflies, Moths, and Other Invertebrates of Costa Rica

NUMBER SIXTY-FIVE, *The Corrie Herring Hooks Series*

Foreword by DANIEL H. JANZEN

Butterflies, Moths, and Other Invertebrates of Costa Rica

A FIELD GUIDE

CARROL L. HENDERSON
with photographs by the author

Illustrations by STEVE ADAMS

UNIVERSITY OF TEXAS PRESS, *Austin*

The University of Texas Press wishes to acknowledge the generous financial support by the following foundations, individuals, and businesses that helped to underwrite the costs of producing the original *Field Guide to the Wildlife of Costa Rica*:

The Dellwood Wildlife Foundation of Dellwood, Minnesota, in memory of wildlife conservationist and founder of the Dellwood Wildlife Foundation, Ramon D. (Ray) Whitney. Ray Whitney was instrumental in helping restore trumpeter swans to Minnesota, and he shared a love and appreciation for the diversity and abundance of wildlife in Costa Rica.

The Costa Rica–Minnesota Foundation of St. Paul, Minnesota, in support of cultural and natural resource initiatives fostering greater understanding, educational programs, and habitat protection for Costa Rica's wildlife.

The late Honorary Consul to Costa Rica from Minnesota and former CEO of the H. B. Fuller Company, Tony Andersen, who was a tireless promoter for cooperative projects of benefit to Costa Rica's culture and environment.

Karen Johnson, President of Preferred Adventures Ltd. of St. Paul, Minnesota, a business that specializes in ecotourism and natural history adventures for worldwide travelers. She has been especially active in promoting wildlife tourism in Costa Rica and other countries of Latin America.

Michael Kaye, President of Costa Rica Expeditions, San José, Costa Rica. Costa Rica Expeditions owns and manages Monteverde Lodge, Tortuguero Lodge, and Corcovado Lodge Tent Camp. This company has set high standards for protecting sensitive tropical habitats while accommodating the needs of nature tourism and adventure travelers in Costa Rica.

Dan Conaway, President of Elegant Adventures, Atlanta, Georgia. Elegant Adventures specializes in quality, customized tours to Latin American destinations, including Costa Rica. This company has served international travelers since its founding in 1986.

Field Guide to the Wildlife of Costa Rica, 2002
Birds of Costa Rica: A Field Guide, 2010
Butterflies, Moths, and Other Invertebrates of Costa Rica: A Field Guide, 2010

Requests for permission to reproduce material from this work should be sent to:
    Permissions
    University of Texas Press
    P.O. Box 7819
    Austin, TX 78713–7819
    www.utexas.edu/utpress/about/bpermission.html

∞ The paper used in this book meets the minimum requirements of ANSI/NISO Z39.48–1992 (R1997) (Permanence of Paper).

LIBRARY OF CONGRESS
CATALOGING-IN-PUBLICATION DATA

Henderson, Carrol L.
Butterflies, moths, and other invertebrates of Costa Rica : a field guide / Carrol L. Henderson ; photographs by Carrol L. Henderson ; illustrations by Steve Adams ; foreword by Daniel H. Janzen. — 1st ed.
    p.   cm. — (The Corrie Herring Hooks series ; no. 65)
    Includes bibliographical references and index.
    ISBN 978-0-292-71966-8 (pbk. : alk. paper)
    1. Butterflies—Costa Rica—Identification. 2. Moths—Costa Rica—Identification. 3. Invertebrates—Costa Rica. I. Title.
    QL553.C67H46 2010
    595.78097286—dc22   2009045571

pg i: Hooded Mantis
pg ii: *Heliconius cydno galanthus*
Facing pg: Backlit canal in Tortuguero National Park

To my wife, Ethelle,
and son and daughter-in-law, Craig and Reem,
with whom I share my love of Costa Rica,
and grandson Mazen Nathaniel,
and to
Drs. George Knaphus, James H. Jenkins, and Daniel H. Janzen,
my mentors.

CONTENTS

FOREWORD

Unless you went there nine thousand years ago, you don't step into the Costa Rican wilderness expecting to be amazed by five-hundred-kilogram beasts (or to be eaten by one of them). And once you have seen one quetzal, you have seen them all. So what is left, then? Well, at least half a million species of little things (diluted here and there by the occasional big tree, noisy gaudy bird, or hopping amphibian). But it is a truly daunting task to get to know this incredible biodiversity, to come to feel at home with all of its many parts, and to understand that most of these small creatures won't bite, poke, cause you to itch, or otherwise incovenience you.

Knowing the insects of Costa Rica is not quite as simple as knowing the common birds or snakes, most of which are already described in great detail on the pages of a guidebook. No, to become familiar with the hundreds of thousands of species of insects and other small things that decorate the Costa Rican wilderness, you have to dive in and let them wash over you. Many—but certainly not all—of the examples caught here by Carrol Henderson's camera you can come to recognize and even learn a name for. Many others will just have to remain a question mark until you capture them with your digital camera, put them out on the Web, and let those who know offer an opinion. Of course there are many resources available on the Web to help you with identification (e.g., http://janzen

Nature tourists looking at the insects attracted to a black light at Rancho Naturalista

.sas.upenn.edu). But this book—which might be subtitled "tales of tropical insect lives"—is a great start.

A curious thing happens in a Costa Rican wildland when you finally slow down and narrow your focus to the little things. You find yourself walking one kilometer in a day instead of the five kilometers that you used to walk. There seems to be something new under every leaf, sitting on every vine, walking under every branch. And if you walk the same trail the next day, the birds are about the same, the plants are the same, but the insects are not. You gradually come to realize how blind we are to the thousands of species of little things. You begin to sense that the

Dr. Dan Janzen, winner of the Crafoord Prize in 1984.

rainforest is not a wall of green but rather a tapestry of creeping, walking, poking, biting, smelling, singing, courting, birthing, and aching life. And every place in the forest is different, every day and every night. The more we recognize, and appreciate, this incredible biodiversity, the more we realize how much it is threatened, and that we are the only ones who can preserve it. If we do not take some really aggressive steps, such as buying it for conservation purposes (http://janzen.sas.upenn.edu/saveit.html), we risk losing it forever.

But another crucial step toward preserving biodiversity is simply getting to know it. So we thank you, Carrol, for broadening your horizons past your beloved feathered microdinosaurs and sharing the results with the rest of us.

DANIEL H. JANZEN
Área de Conservación Guanacaste,
Costa Rica
JULY 8, 2009

PREFACE

I grew up as a farm boy near Zearing in central Iowa, and most of my early travels were within twenty-five miles of our family farm. I had quite a provincial view of life and no concept of ecosystems, biological diversity, or tropical rainforests. I just knew that I loved wildlife. I had no idea that Costa Rica, a small country thousands of miles away in Central America, would later play such a dramatic role in shaping the direction of my personal and professional life.

An early and enthusiastic interest in nature led me to major in zoology and minor in botany at Iowa State University. After completing my bachelor's degree at ISU in 1968, I enrolled in graduate school at the University of Georgia, where I studied ecology, forest and wildlife management, journalism, and public relations. During my search for a thesis topic, Dr. James H. Jenkins directed me to an Organization for Tropical Studies (OTS) course in Costa Rica.

When I began my two-month OTS course in tropical grasslands agriculture in February of 1969, I had no idea it would be such a life-changing experience. Every day was an adventure! I tried to absorb all that I could about the land, the people, and the wildlife of Costa Rica. I quickly learned that this is not a country you can visit just once. By March I had already applied for another OTS course and was subsequently accepted. In June 1969, I drove from Georgia to Costa Rica with Dr. Jenkins for an OTS course in tropical ecology.

The author with an oropendola nest during an OTS course in Costa Rica, 1969.

The OTS faculty, recruited from educational institutions throughout North and Central America, included some of the most notable tropical biologists in the world. They inspired me with their knowledge and enthusiasm about tropical ecosystems. By the end of the tropical ecology course, I had fallen in love with the country, with its people, and with Ethelle González Alvarez, a student at the University of Costa Rica. I returned to Costa Rica a third time in 1969. Ethelle and I were married in December of that year and have now been married forty years. We have a son, Craig, who shares our love and enthusiasm for his Tico heritage, along with his wife, Reem, and son, Mazen Nathaniel.

After returning to the University of Georgia, I wrote my master's thesis, "Fish and Wildlife Resources of Costa Rica, with Notes on Human Influences." The 340-page thesis analyzed human influences that were having significant positive or negative impacts on Costa Rica's wildlife. I also provided recommendations for changes in the game laws that would improve management of the country's wildlife.

In addition to my interest in vertebrates, I had previously studied entomology at Iowa State University and did a National Science Foundation undergraduate research project on mosquitoes under entomologist Dr. Kenneth L. Knight.

During the forty years since my first visit to Costa Rica, I have returned forty-one times. Since 1987, our visits to the country have included leading wildlife tours. Ethelle and I have led twenty-six birding and wildlife tours to Costa Rica since 1987 in coordination with Preferred Adventures Ltd. of St. Paul. We continue to see new species on every visit—and every day is still an adventure!

Each year thousands of first-time tourists are experiencing the same sense of wonder about the country's rainforests and

Every day is an adventure in Costa Rica.

wildlife that I did in 1969, and Costa Rica has become one of the top nature tourism destinations in the world. This book is written to share my enthusiasm and knowledge about the country's wildlife with those tourists and with Costa Ricans who share our love of nature. It is written to answer questions about identification, distribution, natural history, and the incredible ecological adaptations of many wildlife species. It also provides the opportunity to recognize the people and conservation programs that have made Costa Rica a world leader in preserving its tropical forest and wildlife resources. This is not a typical field guide. It includes selected species of butterflies, moths, and other invertebrates that are likely to catch the attention of tourists in Costa Rica because of their conspicuous colors, size, or unique life histories. It does not cover the invertebrates comprehensively, but it will assist in identifying many of the more common creatures that are likely to be encountered during a visit at the peak of the annual tourist season, from January through March.

Caligo atreus

ACKNOWLEDGMENTS

Writing this book has been a real labor of love. It represents the culmination of forty years of personal and professional relationships in Costa Rica. Special appreciation goes to my wife, Ethelle, and my son, Craig, who have traveled with me from Minnesota to Costa Rica many times and helped with everything from wildlife observations to editing and preparing the manuscript. In 1985, Karen Johnson, the owner of Preferred Adventures Ltd. in St. Paul, Minnesota, urged us to try leading a birding trip to Costa Rica. We finally agreed and led our first trip in 1987. It was the beginning of a wonderful experience that has enabled us to meet many special people in our tour groups as well as Costa Rican tourism outfitters, guides, and ecolodge staffs.

Michael Kaye, the owner of Costa Rica Expeditions, has been very supportive of this project and has coordinated our travel there. He facilitated travel to visit several sites for photography purposes, including Monteverde Lodge. Carlos Gómez Nieto is the extraordinary guide who has led all but one of our Costa Rican birding trips. Carlos is the premier birder in Costa Rica, and his vast knowledge of wildlife behavior and identification has helped us accumulate our wildlife records, which now exceed 27,000 observations. Manuel Salas and Marco Antonio "Niño" Morales have been the drivers for most of our trips and have been invaluable in spotting birds and in providing us with safe and memorable travel experiences.

Other people have helped with facilitating our travels and the collection of information and photos. They include Lisa and Kathy Erb at Rancho Naturalista; Don Efraín Chacón, Rolando Chacón, and the rest of the Chacón family; Amos Bien of Rara Avis; Gail Hewson-Hull; Luis Diego Gómez; and the late Dr. Alexander Skutch and Pamela Skutch at Los Cusingos.

Biologists and scientists provided expertise on species identification and life history data, including Dr. Daniel Janzen, Dr. Graciela Candelas, Dr. Alexander Skutch, Dr. Frank T. Hovore, and Jorge Corrales of the Instituto Nacional de Biodiversidad (INBIO).

And finally, special appreciation goes to all the Costa Rican travelers who have accompanied us on our birding trips and provided the companionship, sharp eyes, and friendships that have enriched our lives.

Butterflies, Moths,and Other Invertebrates of Costa Rica

The name "Costa Rica" means "Rich Coast."

INTRODUCTION

Costa Rica! The name generates a sense of excitement and anticipation among international travelers. Among European explorers, the first recorded visitor was Christopher Columbus in 1502. On his fourth trip to the New World, Columbus landed where the port city of Limón is now located. The natives he encountered wore golden disks around their necks. He called this new place "Costa Rica," meaning "Rich Coast," because he thought the gold came from there. The gold had actually come from other countries and had been obtained as a trade item from native traders along the coast.

Spanish treasure seekers eventually discovered their error and went elsewhere in their quest for gold. The irony is that Christopher Columbus actually picked the perfect name for this country. The wealth overlooked by the Spaniards is the rich biological diversity that includes more than 505,000 species of plants and wildlife. That species richness is an incredible natural resource that sustains one of the most successful nature tourism industries in the Western Hemisphere. It also provides the basis for a newly evolving biodiversity industry of "chemical prospecting" among plants and creatures, in search of new foods and medicines for humans.

For such a small country, Costa Rica gets much well-deserved international attention and has become one of the most popular nature tourism destinations in the Americas. The lure is not "sun and sand"

experiences at big hotels on the country's beaches; it is unspoiled nature in far-flung nooks and crannies of tropical wildlands that are accessible at rustic, locally owned nature lodges throughout the country.

It is now possible to immerse yourself in the biological wealth of tropical forests during a vacation in Costa Rica. During a two-week visit you may see more than three hundred to four hundred species of birds, mammals, reptiles, amphibians, butterflies, moths, and other invertebrates. Some vacations are planned for rest and relaxation, but who can do that in such a diverse country where there is so much nature to see and experience? In Costa Rica, every day is an adventure, and the marvelous diversity and abundance of wildlife create an enthusiasm for nature that many people have not experienced since childhood.

The ease with which it is possible to travel to Costa Rica and enjoy wildlife in

Costa Rican tourist DeWayne Jackson, photographing a Caligo butterfly.

such a pristine setting makes a visitor think it has always been that way. It has not. The appealing travel and tourism conditions are the product of nearly four decades of social, educational, and cultural developments.

There was a time when Costa Rican wildlife was persecuted at every opportunity. Virtually every creature weighing over a pound was shot for its value as meat or for its hide. Wildlife was killed year-round from the time of settlement through the 1960s. Instead of acquiring souvenirs like T-shirts and postcards in those days, Costa Rican visitors in the 1960s found vendors selling boa constrictor hides, caiman-skin briefcases, stuffed caimans, skins of spotted cats, and sea turtle eggs.

HISTORICAL PERSPECTIVE

To appreciate the abundance of today's wildlife populations, it is necessary to understand the revolution in wildlife conservation and habitat preservation that has occurred since the 1960s. Dozens of dedicated biologists, politicians, and private citizens have contributed to Costa Rica's world leadership in tropical forest conservation, wildlife protection, and nature tourism over the past fifty-plus years. This process occurred in five phases: (1) Research, (2) Education, (3) Preservation, (4) Conservation, and (5) Nature Tourism.

Research

One of the earliest advances for Costa Rica's legacy of conservation was the development of research data on Costa Rica's plants and wildlife. Without such basic knowledge, there can be little appreciation, respect, or protection for wild species. In 1941, Dr. Alexander Skutch homesteaded property in the San Isidro del General Valley along the Río Peña Blanca. After settling there with his wife, Pamela, Dr. Skutch studied Costa Rica's birds for more than sixty years and continued to observe them and record their life history in his prolific writings until his passing in 2004.

In 1954, another biologist, Dr. Archie Carr, started epic research. Dr. Carr, from the University of Florida, began a lifelong commitment to the protection and management of the green turtle at Tortuguero. That effort continues to this day, thanks to his son, Dr. David Carr, and the work of the Caribbean Conservation Corporation, which was created in 1959.

Another significant development for Costa Rica's legacy of leadership in tropical research was the creation of the Tropical Science Center. It was founded in 1962 by Drs. Leslie R. Holdridge, Joseph A. Tosi, and Robert J. Hunter. These three scientists promoted research on tropical ecosystems, land use, and sustainable development. Dr. Gary Hartshorn later joined the staff to add more expertise in the development of tropical forest management strategies. The Tropical Science Center was instrumental in establishing La Selva Biological Field Station and the Monteverde Cloud Forest Reserve and in preserving Los Cusingos, the forest reserve formerly owned by Dr. Alexander Skutch. That reserve is now managed by the Tropical Science Center.

Another research catalyst for subsequent conservation and land protection was the creation of the Organization for Tropical Studies (OTS) in 1964. The OTS is a consortium of fifty-five universities and educational institutions throughout the Americas. The OTS operates three tropical research field stations—located at La Selva, Palo Verde, and San Vito. Tropical biologists from throughout the world come to these field stations to pursue pioneering

Dr. Dan Janzen teaching an ots course in 1967. Photo provided courtesy of the Organization for Tropical Studies.

studies on taxonomy, ecology, and conservation of tropical ecosystems.

For many decades, people had believed it was necessary to eliminate tropical forests in the name of progress, to create croplands, pastures, and monocultures of exotic trees for the benefit of society. Tropical biologists of the ots changed the way people viewed tropical forests and helped society realize the infinitely greater ecological, climatic, and economic benefits that can accrue from preserving and managing tropical forests as sustainable resources.

Education

In 1963 the National Science Foundation supported the Advanced Science Seminar in Tropical Biology, which was subsequently adapted by ots. The ots initiated a second part of its legacy with field courses in tropical ecology, forestry, agriculture, and land use for undergraduate and graduate students from throughout the Americas. Since its founding, the ots has conducted more than 200 field courses for at least 3,600 students. For many of these students, including the author, the courses were life-changing experiences. The faculty who taught these courses were some of the most prominent ecologists in the world, including, among others, Drs. Dan Janzen, Mildred Mathias, Carl Rettenmeyer, Frank Barnwell, Rafael Lucas Rodríguez Caballero, Gordon Orions, Roy McDiarmid, Larry Wolf, and Rex Daubenmire.

Another significant source of tropical education and research has been the Tropical Agricultural Center for Research and Education (Centro Agronómico Tropical de Investigación y Enseñanza; CATIE). This center was created in 1942 at Turrialba and was originally known as the Interamerican Institute of Agricultural Science (Instituto Interamericano de Ciencias Agrícolas; IICA). Graduate students come from all over Latin America to study agriculture, forestry, and wildlife management there.

Preservation

By the 1960s, about 50 percent of Costa Rica's forests had been cut, and the clearing continued. It became apparent that national programs for protection of the remaining forests and wildlife would be necessary if they were to be preserved into the next century.

Logging in Costa Rica, 1969.

The first wildlife conservation law was decreed on July 20, 1961, and was updated with bylaws on June 7, 1965. These laws and regulations provided for the creation and enforcement of game laws, the establishment of wildlife refuges, the prohibition of commercial sale of wildlife products, the issuance of hunting and fishing licenses, the establishment of fines for violations, and the creation of restrictions on the export and import of wildlife. Complete protection was given to tapirs, manatees, White-tailed Deer does accompanied by fawns, and Resplendent Quetzals. The laws, however, were not enforced.

In 1968, a Costa Rican graduate student, Mario Boza, was inspired by a visit to the Great Smoky Mountains National Park. In 1969 a Forestry Protection Law allowed national parks to be established, and Mario Boza was designated as the only employee of the new National Parks Department. He wrote a master plan for the newly designated Poás Volcano National Park as his master's thesis subject.

In 1970, wildlife laws were still being ignored by poachers, and wildlife continued to disappear. President "Don Pepe" Figueres visited Dr. Archie Carr and graduate student David Ehrenfeld to see the green turtle nesting beaches at Tortuguero. He was considering a proposal to protect the area as a national park. The following account was later written by Dr. David Ehrenfeld (1989):

> It was Don Pepe's first visit to the legendary Tortuguero—we had been watching a green turtle nest, also a first for him. El Presidente, a short, Napoleonic man with boundless energy, was enjoying himself enormously. Both he and Archie were truly charismatic people, and they liked and respected one another.

> The rest of us went along quietly, enjoying the show. As we walked up the beach towards the boca, where the Río Tortuguero meets the sea, Don Pepe questioned Dr. Carr about the green turtles and their need for conservation. How important was it to make Tortuguero a sanctuary? Just then, a flashlight picked out a strange sight up ahead.

> A turtle was on the beach, near the waterline, trailing something. And behind her was a line of eggs which, for some reason, she was depositing on the bare, unprotected sand. We hurried to see what the problem was.

> When we got close, it was all too apparent. The entire undershell of the turtle had been cut away by poachers who were after calipee, or cartilage, to dry and sell to the European turtle soup manufacturers. Not interested in the meat or eggs, they had evidently then flipped her back on her belly for sport, to see where she would crawl. What she was trailing was her intestines. The poachers had probably been frightened away by our lights only minutes before.

> Dr. Carr, who knew sea turtles better than any human being on earth and who had devoted much of his life to their protection, said nothing. He looked at Don Pepe, and so did I. It was a moment of revelation. Don Pepe was very, very angry, trembling with rage. This was his country, his place. He had risked his life for it fighting in the Cerro de la Muerte. The turtles were part of this place, even part of its name: Tortuguero; . . . She was home, laying her eggs for the last time.

Don Pepe realized that the ancient turtles, as well as the Costa Rican people, needed a safe place to live and raise their young. The poaching had to end. He declared

Rainbow over the Monteverde Cloud Forest Reserve.

Tortuguero National Park by executive decree in 1970. The tragic poaching incident with the nesting green turtle was probably the pivotal incident that catalyzed the national parks movement in Costa Rica. Mario Boza served under President Figueres as the National Park Service director from 1970 to 1974. By the end of 1974, the service had grown to an organization of 100 employees with an annual budget of $600,000. A total of 2.5 percent of the country was designated as national parks and reserves.

Private preservation efforts also began in the 1970s. Scientists George and Harriet Powell and Monteverde resident Wilford Guindon created the 810-acre Monteverde Cloud Forest Reserve. They brought in the Tropical Science Center to own and manage the preserve, which now totals 27,428 acres. The Monteverde Conservation League was subsequently formed to help manage and carry out conservation projects and land acquisition.

In 1984, Dr. Dan Janzen brought more international recognition to Costa Rica when he received the Crafoord Prize in Coevolutionary Ecology from the Swedish Royal Academy of Sciences. This is the ecologist's equivalent of the Nobel Prize. Dr. Janzen received the prize for his pioneering research on entomology and ecology of tropical dry forests. This focused attention on the need for preserving tropical dry forests in the Guanacaste Conservation Area (http://www.acguanacaste.ac.cr).

Oscar Arias was elected president in 1986. He created the Ministry of Energy, Mining, and Natural Resources (MIRENEM) by merging the national land management departments to make them more efficient in managing the nation's natural resources. That agency is now referred to as the Ministry of Environment and Energy (Ministerio del Ambiente y Energía; MINAE).

Since then, Costa Rica's national system

Dr. Rodrigo Gámez, parataxonomist and director general of INBIO.

882 birds, 236 mammals, 228 reptiles, 178 amphibians, 360,000 insects, and 10,000 plants. This represents about 5 percent of the world's species. So far, about 90,000 of those species have been described, and INBIO's collections include 3.5 million specimens.

Following the creation of INBIO, MIRENEM developed a national system of "conservation areas" in 1990. This is referred to as SINAC (Sistema Nacional de Areas de Conservación). Eleven conservation areas were established. Personnel in the fields of wildlife, forestry, parks, and agriculture teamed up to manage the national parks and wildlands in each conservation area. Their goal is the conservation of Costa Rica's biodiversity for nondestructive use by Costa Ricans and the world populace. This national scale of ecosystem-based management predated efforts in more "developed" countries by years.

of parks and reserves has continued to grow and mature. It now consists of 161 protected areas, including twenty-five national parks. Those areas total 3,221,635 acres—almost 26 percent of the country's land area. More information on the national park system can be found at www.costarica-nationalparks.com.

Conservation

As the national park system grew and encompassed more life zones, it became clear to ecological visionaries like Dr. Dan Janzen and Dr. Rodrigo Gámez Lobo that they had an opportunity to take another bold step that would place them in a world-leadership role for conservation of biological diversity and creation of economic benefits to society from that biological diversity. They created the National Biodiversity Institute (Instituto Nacional de Biodiversidad; INBIO). Dr. Gámez Lobo became the first director of INBIO and continues his leadership as president of INBIO. The ambitious goal of this institute was to collect, identify, and catalog all of the living species in Costa Rica. Estimated at 505,000 species, this figure includes

Nature Tourism

Beginning in the mid-1980s, and concurrent with the conservation phase, the value of Costa Rica's national parks (NPS), national wildlife refuges (NWRS), and biological reserves (BRS) was reaffirmed in another way: as a resource for nature tourism. Nature tourism is motivated by the desire to experience unspoiled nature: to see, enjoy, experience, or photograph scenery, natural communities, wildlife, and native plants. The first rule of nature tourism is that wildlife is worth more alive—in the wild—than dead. It has become a great incentive to protect wildlife from poachers and to conserve the forests as habitat for the wildlife.

Nature tourism provided new employment opportunities for Costa Ricans as travel agency personnel, outfitters, nature lodge owners and staff, drivers, and naturalist guides. The best naturalist guides can identify birds, mammals, reptiles, amphibians, flowers, butterflies, and trees. These dedicated guides share an infectious enthusiasm for the country as they help visitors experience hundreds of species during a visit. Guides like Carlos Gómez Nieto have seen more than 730 of the country's bird species and can identify most of them by sight and sound.

Rainforests—especially the international loss of rainforests—received a great deal of publicity in the 1980s. Costa Rica's national parks provided an opportunity to attract tourists to experience the mystique and beauty of those forests. Improved road systems and small airstrips throughout the country provided access to those parks and private reserves in the rainforests. Enterprising outfitters recognized the opportunity to establish locally owned and managed nature tourism lodges to cater to this new breed of international tourists.

One of the best-known pioneers in nature-based tourism is Michael Kaye. Originally from New York, he was a white-water rafting outfitter in the Grand Canyon before he founded Costa Rica Expeditions in 1985. In Costa Rica he provides tourists with the opportunity for

Birding guide Carlos Gómez Nieto.

adventure tourism, including white-water rafting and wildlife viewing. Kaye built three lodges—Tortuga, Monteverde, and Corcovado—and he provided ecologically based innovations and adaptations at these facilities that minimized their impact on the environment and sensitized visitors to the importance and vulnerability of the forests where these lodges were located. Kaye believes that tourists respond to world-class facilities and services that are provided by local ownership and management of smaller, dispersed lodging facilities. Costa Rica's tourism forte is that it is one of the best rainforest destinations in the Americas because it is safe and easily accessible; the attraction is not the beaches where huge hotels are owned by corporations from other countries.

There are now dozens of other locally owned nature-based lodges throughout the country. John Aspinall founded Costa Rica Sun Tours and built the Arenal Observatory Lodge. His brother Peter founded Tiskita Jungle Lodge. Don Perry initiated the Rainforest Aerial Tram facility. John and Kathleen Erb founded Rancho Naturalista and Tárcol Lodge. John and Karen Lewis founded Lapa Ríos. Other local nature lodges are Selva Verde, El Gavilán, Hacienda Solimar, La Pacifica, Caño Negro Lodge, La Ensenada, Villa Lapas, Rancho Casa Grande, Rara Avis, Savegre Mountain Lodge, Bosque de Paz, Drake Bay Wilderness Resort, and El Pizote Lodge. OTS research facilities like La Selva and San Vito also provide accommodations for nature tourists.

International connections also benefited Costa Rica's nature tourism. In 1989, Preferred Adventures Ltd. was founded by Karen Johnson in St. Paul, Minnesota, with special emphasis on Costa Rican tourism. Through the efforts of Karen

Ctenosaur sharing the beach with tourists, Tamarindo.

Johnson and the late Tony Andersen, Chairman of the Board and former CEO of the H. B. Fuller Company and Honorary Consul to Costa Rica from Minnesota, these connections resulted in the creation of the Costa Rica–Minnesota Foundation, which has promoted cultural, medical, and conservation projects in Costa Rica.

As nature tourism lodges proliferated after the mid-1980s, the number of tourists arriving in Costa Rica grew steadily. In 1988, about 330,000 tourists came, and over the next eleven years the number increased to 1,027,000 people per year. By 2006, the number of tourists had risen to 1,716,000. From 1988 to 2006, the annual number of national park visitors increased from about 865,600 to 1,205,100, and the number of tour operators increased from 58 to 325. All of this is happening in an area only one-fourth the size of Minnesota.

Nature tourism has turned heads throughout Costa Rica and Latin America because of the amount of income it has generated. In 1991, tourism contributed $330 million to the Costa Rican national economy. By 1999 that figure had increased to $940 million and exceeded the amount generated by exports of coffee ($408 million) and bananas ($566 million)! By 2006, tourism income exceeded one billion dollars: $1,620,800,000. In addition, nature tourism created more than 140,000 jobs.

The best thing about nature tourism is that when it is practiced ethically and in balance with the environment, it is a sustainable natural resource use that diversifies the economic base of the country and makes the value of the national parks and wildlife resources obvious to the citizenry.

Costa Ricans now realize that a significant part of the economic health and prosperity of their country is tied to the health and prosperity of their national parks, forests, and wildlife and to the future of the country's macaws, quetzals, tepescuintles, Jaguars, and Green Turtles. Don Pepe Figueres was right. If you make the world a safe place for green turtles and other wildlife, it becomes a better place for people, too.

GEOGRAPHY

Costa Rica, a Central American country between Panama and Nicaragua, is shown in Figure 1. Considering its relatively small size, 19,653 square miles, Costa Rica has an exceptionally high diversity of plants and wildlife, more than half a million species. This is explained in part by the fascinating geological history of the region.

The geological history that led to the creation of Costa Rica goes back about 200 million years to the Triassic Period, when much of the earth's landmass was composed of a supercontinent called Pangaea. The supercontinent began to separate through continental drift, portrayed in Figure 2, which is the process by which the earth's landmasses essentially float on the molten core of the earth, drift among the oceans, and occasionally separate or merge. Pangaea eventually separated into two supercontinents. The northern supercontinent, called Laurasia, later became North

Figure 1. Location of Costa Rica in Central America.

America, Asia, and Europe. The southern portion, called Gondwanaland, drifted apart and later became South America, Africa, southern Asia, and Australia.

About 130 million years ago the western portion of Gondwanaland began to separate into South America and Africa. Concurrently, the North American landmass drifted westward from the European landmass. Both North America and South America drifted westward, but they were still separate. By the Pliocene Period, about three to four million years ago, North America and South America were aligned from north to south, but a gap in the ocean floor between the two continents existed where southern Nicaragua, Costa Rica, and Panama are today.

About three million years ago an undersea plate of the earth's crust, called a tectonic plate, began moving north and eastward in the Pacific Ocean into the

Highway map of Costa Rica. Source: U.S. State Department.

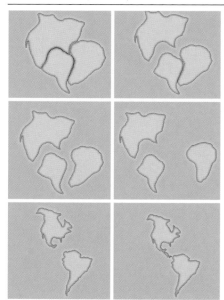

Figure 2. Stages in the process of continental drift that led to the creation of Costa Rica.

area between North and South America. This particular tectonic plate, the Cocos Plate, pushed onto the Caribbean Plate and rose above sea level to create the land bridge that now connects North and South America. That bridge became southern Nicaragua, Costa Rica, and the central and western portions of Panama.

BIOGEOGRAPHY

Biogeography is the relationship between the geography of a region and the long-term distribution and dispersal patterns of its plants and wildlife. The geological history of Costa Rica, Nicaragua, and Panama created a situation in which they became a land bridge between two continents. Plants and wildlife have been dispersing across that bridge for the last three million years; as a result, Costa Rica became a biological mixing bowl of species from both continents. Those dispersal patterns are shown in Figure 3.

Temperate-climate plants that have dispersed southward from North America include alders (*Alnus*), oaks (*Quercus*), walnuts (*Juglans*), magnolias (*Magnolia*), blueberries (*Vaccinium*), Indian paintbrush (*Castilleja*), and mistletoe (*Gaiadendron*). Most dispersal appears to have occurred during cooler glacial periods. As the climate became warmer, these northern-origin plants became biologically stranded on the mountains, where the climate was cooler.

Wildlife dispersing from North America across the land bridge included coyotes, tapirs, deer, jaguars, squirrels, and bears. Birds that dispersed from North America to Central and South America included wrens, thrushes, sparrows, woodpeckers, and common dippers.

Plants that dispersed from South America toward the north included tree ferns, cycads, heliconias, bromeliads, orchids, poor-man's umbrella (*Gunnera*), *Puja,* and *Espeletia*. Wildlife that dispersed northward from South America through Costa Rica are opossums, armadillos, porcupines, sloths, monkeys, anteaters, agoutis, and tepescuintles. Some species expanded through Central America and Mexico to

Topographical relief map of Costa Rica.

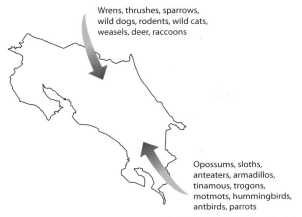

Wrens, thrushes, sparrows,
wild dogs, rodents, wild cats,
weasels, deer, raccoons

Opossums, sloths,
anteaters, armadillos,
tinamous, trogons,
motmots, hummingbirds,
antbirds, parrots

Figure 3. Costa Rica became a land bridge that facilitated the dispersal of wildlife from both North and South America.

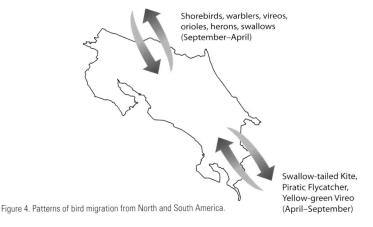

Shorebirds, warblers, vireos,
orioles, herons, swallows
(September–April)

Swallow-tailed Kite,
Piratic Flycatcher,
Yellow-green Vireo
(April–September)

Figure 4. Patterns of bird migration from North and South America.

the United States. Birds that dispersed from South America to Costa Rica and beyond include tinamous, hummingbirds, motmots, trogons, spinetails, flowerpiercers, antbirds, parrots, and woodcreepers. Likewise, insects have dispersed from both the north and south into Costa Rica.

Migratory Species

NORTHERN HEMISPHERE MIGRANTS

Among Costa Rica's 882 bird species, about 180 are migratory. Most migrate from North America to winter in Latin America between September and April. Patterns of migration from the north and south are shown in Figure 4.

The story behind the migratory traditions and the origins of these migrants is both intriguing and surprising. Migratory birds are believed to have originated in the tropics. In tropical forests, insects are present in a great diversity of species, but the numbers of any one species are low. They can be very difficult for birds to find in adequate quantities to feed young. That is why the parents of many tropical bird species have young from previous broods that help feed their young. In northern temperate forests, the species diversity of insects is lower, but the seasonal abundance of each species can be great—as occurs in outbreaks of tent caterpillars. This is referred to as a "protein pulse" as it relates to bird food provided by insects. Such a bountiful supply of insects provides ideal conditions for parent birds to reproduce and adequately feed their young. The annual pattern of seasonal migration was likely tied to the passing of glacial periods, when mild northern summers and the increasing presence and abundance of northern insects benefited birds that migrated north to nest.

Among butterflies, the Monarch is famous for its international migrations between North America and Mexico, but it does not migrate to Costa Rica. The Monarchs there are nonmigratory. Some butterflies and moths in Costa Rica undergo irregular mass migrations that are mostly a one-way phenomenon. Perhaps the most conspicuous of these are the irregular cross-country migrations of an iridescent green page moth, *Urania fulgens*. Most of these movements occur within the country, but some species, like the Black Witch moth (*Ascalapha odorata*), can move northward into the United States.

SOUTHERN HEMISPHERE MIGRANTS

As most northern migrants are leaving for North America in March and April, a few birds are migrating from South America to Costa Rica to stay from April through September. The Swallow-tailed Kite, Piratic Flycatcher, Blue-and-white Swallow, and Yellow-green Vireo are migrants from South America.

ELEVATIONAL MIGRANTS

Some resident birds, butterflies, and moths in Costa Rica, like the Three-wattled Bellbird, *Mechanitis polymnia isthmia*, *Greta morgane oto*, *Marpesia merops*, *Marpesia coresia*, and *Marpesia chiron*, migrate each year along an elevational gradient. For example, the Three-wattled Bellbird moves from breeding areas in middle- and high-elevation "temperate" forests during the rainy season (April through December) to lower-elevation "tropical" forests during the dry season (January

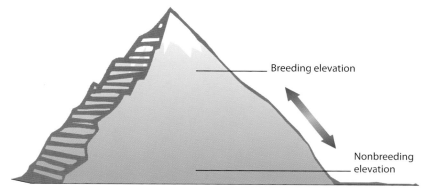

Figure 5. Some tropical insects and birds, like the Three-wattled Bellbird, carry out elevational migrations between breeding seasons and nonbreeding seasons.

through March), as illustrated in Figure 5. The Silver-throated Tanager, the Scarlet-thighed Dacnis, and many Costa Rican butterflies and moths carry out elevational migrations.

ENDEMIC SPECIES

An endemic species is one found in one country or region and nowhere else in the world. Costa Rica has three zones of endemism, in which unique species and subspecies are found. These zones occur because geographic barriers created by mountains, arid zones, or oceans have isolated a particular population from the rest of its species, and eventually they evolve into separate species through natural selection.

Endemic Wildlife of the Highlands

The mountain ranges and volcanoes of Costa Rica and western Panama include only about 160 species of birds out of the 882 species present in the country. The same holds true for insect species and subspecies; their diversity is reduced as the elevation increases. The concept of endemism is often applied to species in a single country, but in the case of the Costa Rican highlands, where the Talamanca Mountains are contiguous with those of western Panama, the area of endemism crosses the border. For example, *Heliconius clysonymus montanus* and *Hypanartia dione arcaei* are regional endemic species of the highlands in the Talamanca Mountains of Costa Rica and adjacent mountains of Panama. For the purposes of this book, it is considered a single endemic zone. Many butterflies have evolved into distinctive species or subspecies because they were reproductively isolated from other populations of the same species

Figure 6. Highland zone of endemic species in Costa Rica and western Panama.

or similar species in the mountains of Guatemala and southern Mexico and in the mountains of eastern Panama and Colombia. This highland endemic zone is portrayed in Figure 6.

Endemic Species of the Southern Pacific Lowlands

Costa Rica's mountain ranges serve as a giant barrier that separates moist and wet lowland rainforest species that originally dispersed from South America to both the Caribbean lowlands and the southern Pacific lowlands. The mountains have caused reproductive isolation between populations of species that occurred in both areas. Over geologic time, the species diverged into separate species. This has contributed to a second zone of endemism in Costa Rica, the southern Pacific lowlands. There are several interesting pairs of species that have a common ancestor but have been separated from each other by the mountains between the Caribbean

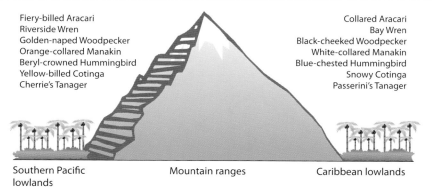

Fiery-billed Aracari
Riverside Wren
Golden-naped Woodpecker
Orange-collared Manakin
Beryl-crowned Hummingbird
Yellow-billed Cotinga
Cherrie's Tanager

Collared Aracari
Bay Wren
Black-cheeked Woodpecker
White-collared Manakin
Blue-chested Hummingbird
Snowy Cotinga
Passerini's Tanager

Southern Pacific lowlands

Mountain ranges

Caribbean lowlands

Figure 7. Closely related pairs of allopatric species of the Caribbean and Pacific lowlands that share a common ancestor but are now separated by Costa Rica's mountains.

lowlands and the southern Pacific lowlands, as shown in Figure 7. Since the range of one species does not overlap the range of the other species in the pair, these are referred to as allopatric species.

This divergence of two species from a common ancestor is a continuing process, as evidenced by the recent decision by taxonomists to split the Scarlet-rumped Tanager into two species, Cherrie's Tanager in the Pacific lowlands and Passerini's Tanager in the Caribbean lowlands. The males are identical, but the females are distinctive. Other birds designated as endemic subspecies include the Masked Yellowthroat (Chiriquí race) and the Variable Seedeater (Pacific race). One day they may eventually become different enough from the Caribbean subspecies to be designated as new species.

Additional endemic species of the southern Pacific lowlands that do not have a corresponding closely related species in the Caribbean lowlands include Baird's Trogon, Black-cheeked Ant-Tanager, Granular Poison Dart Frog, Mangrove Hummingbird, *Heliconius ismenius clarescens*, and Red-backed Squirrel Monkey.

Endemic Species of Cocos Island

A third zone of endemism is Cocos Island. This island is 600 miles out in the Pacific, and three endemic birds have evolved there: Cocos Finch, Cocos Cuckoo, and Cocos Flycatcher. Cocos Island is an extension of the Galápagos Island archipelago but it is owned by Costa Rica. There are thirteen finches on the Galápagos Islands commonly referred to as Darwin's finches. The Cocos Finch is actually the fourteenth Darwin's finch. Undoubtedly, a variety of invertebrates are endemic to this island also.

Endemic Species and DNA Barcoding Revelations

The previous discussion of endemic species applies best to birds. The dynamic and changing taxonomic status of many butterflies, moths, and other insects, however, is a fascinating phenomenon that goes beyond traditional geographic barriers as a driving force behind natural selection and the creation of new species. The evolution of new species from a common

Dan Janzen with parataxonomist Osvaldo Espinoza of the Guanacaste Conservation area.

Astraptes fulgerator.

ancestor can occur as a species diverges to utilize different host plant species across the range of the common ancestor. The pioneering work by Dr. Dan Janzen and the *gusaneros* (parataxonomists) of the Guanacaste Conservation Area has contributed to the development of a research tool called DNA barcoding.

The analysis of mitochondrial DNA from moths and butterflies in the Guanacaste Conservation Area has revealed that some insects that were formerly considered a single species actually belong to a closely related group of separate but similar-looking species that depend on different host plants. For example, a colorful and conspicuous skipper butterfly formerly called *Astraptes fulgerator* is found from Texas to Argentina. DNA barcoding analysis of host plant use has revealed that this butterfly is now ten different species that all look very similar. Many of these new species could potentially be considered as endemic, but that title is not relevant at this point because more research is needed; the new species have not yet been assigned scientific names, and they have no common names.

MAJOR BIOLOGICAL ZONES

The most detailed and traditional classification of the habitats in Costa Rica includes twelve "life zones," as described by the late Dr. Leslie Holdridge of the Tropical Science Center. Those life zones are based on average annual precipitation, average annual temperature, and evapotranspiration potential. Evapotranspiration potential involves the relative amount of humidity or aridity of a region.

For tourism planning purposes, that classification system has been simplified in this book from twelve to six biological zones. These zones, the first five of which are shown in Figure 8, coincide with the distribution of many Costa Rican wildlife species and are designed for trip planning by wildlife tourists. The sixth zone consists of the entire coastline of both the Pacific and the Caribbean coasts. A good trip itinerary should include at least three biological zones in addition to the Central Plateau.

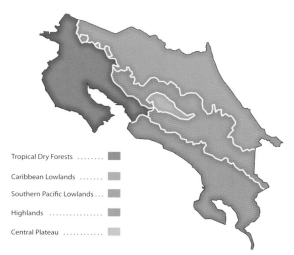

Tropical Dry Forests .... ■

Caribbean Lowlands .... ■

Southern Pacific Lowlands ... ■

Highlands .... ■

Central Plateau .... ■

Figure 8. Five biological zones of Costa Rica. In addition, the country's entire coastline, beaches, and mangrove lagoons make up a sixth zone of biological importance.

Tropical dry forest in Guanacaste.

Tropical Dry Forest

The tropical dry forest in northwestern Costa Rica is a lowland region that generally coincides with the boundaries of Guanacaste Province. It extends eastward to the Cordilleras of Guanacaste and Tilarán, southeast to Carara NP, and north to the Nicaragua border. This zone extends from sea level to approximately 2,000 feet in elevation.

This region is characterized by a pronounced dry season from December through March. The deciduous trees include many plants that lose their leaves

Southern Pacific lowland forest, Manuel Antonio National Park.

during the dry season and flower during that leafless period. Common trees are bullhorn acacia (*Acacia*), *Tabebuia,* strangler fig (*Ficus*), *Guazuma,* kapok (*Ceiba*), *Bombacopsis,* buttercup tree (*Cochlospermum*), *Anacardium,* and the national tree of Costa Rica, the Guanacaste tree (*Enterolobium cyclocarpum*). The tallest trees approach 100 feet in height. Rainfall ranges from 40 to 80 inches per year.

Epiphytes are not a major component of the dry forest canopy, as they are in the moist and wet forests. However, some trees are thickly covered with vines like monkey vine (*Bauhinia*) and *Combretum.* The ease with which this forest can be burned and cleared for agricultural purposes has made the tropical dry forest the most endangered habitat in the country.

An important habitat within the dry forest consists of the riparian forests along the rivers, also called gallery forests. They maintain more persistent foliage during the dry season.

Wetlands, estuaries, islands, and backwaters of this region's rivers are also a major habitat for wetland wildlife. Especially important are lands along the Río Tempisque, its tributaries, and the wetlands of Palo Verde NP. Important examples of tropical dry forest habitat are preserved in Guanacaste Province; Santa Rosa, Las Baulas, and Palo Verde NPs; and Lomas Barbudal BR. The southeastern limit of this region is at Carara NP, which has a combination of wildlife characteristic of both the dry forest and the southern Pacific lowlands.

Southern Pacific Lowlands

The southern Pacific lowlands include the moist and wet forested region from Carara NP through the General Valley, Osa Peninsula, and Golfo Dulce lowlands to the Panama border and inland to the premontane forest zone at San Vito las Cruces.

The moist and wet forests of this region receive 80 to 200 inches of rainfall per year, with a more pronounced dry season from December through March than occurs in the Caribbean lowlands. These forests have fewer epiphytes than are found in Caribbean lowland forests. The tallest trees exceed 150 feet in height.

Among tree species are the kapok (*Ceiba*), *Anacardium,* strangler fig (*Ficus*), wild almond (*Terminalia*), purpleheart

Central Plateau overlooking San José and suburbs.

(*Peltogyne purpurea*), *Carapa,* buttercup tree (*Cochlospermum vitifolium*), *Virola,* balsa (*Ochroma*), milk tree (*Brosimum*), *Raphia,* garlic tree (*Caryocar costaricense*), and *Hura*. Understory plants include species like bullhorn acacia (*Acacia*), walking palm (*Socratea*), *Bactris,* and *Heliconia*. Most trees maintain their foliage throughout the year.

Much of this region has been converted to pastureland and plantations of pineapple, coconut, and African oil palm. Among the most significant reserves remaining in natural habitat are Carara, Manuel Antonio, and Corcovado NPs. Corcovado NP is one of the finest examples of lowland wet forest in Central America, and it has excellent populations of rainforest wildlife. Additional private reserves include one near San Isidro del General at Los Cusingos, the former home of Dr. Alexander and Pamela Skutch. It is now managed by the Tropical Science Center. The Wilson Botanical Garden at San Vito is an excellent example of premontane wet forest and is owned and operated by

the Organization for Tropical Studies. The southern Pacific lowland area is of biological interest because it is the northernmost range limit for some South American species.

Premontane (middle-elevation) sites like the Wilson Botanical Garden at San Vito are included in this biological region because many of the species typical of this region are found up to about 4,000 feet along the western slopes of the Talamanca Mountains. Premontane forests, like those preserved at the Wilson Botanical Garden, are the second most endangered life zone in Costa Rica, after tropical dry forests.

Central Plateau (Central Valley)

The Central Plateau contains the human population center of Costa Rica. The capital, San José, and adjoining suburbs are located in this relatively flat plateau at an elevation of approximately 3,900 feet. It is bordered on the north and east by major volcanoes of the Central Cordillera: Barva, Irazú, Poás, and Turrialba. To the south is the northern end of the Talamanca Mountains.

Rainfall ranges from 40 to 80 inches per year, and the original life zone in this area was premontane moist forest, but that forest has been largely cleared. The climate of the region, about 68 degrees Fahrenheit year-round, made it ideal for human settlement, and the rich volcanic soils made it an excellent region for growing coffee and sugarcane. The region is also important for production of fruits, vegetables, and horticultural export products like ferns and flowers.

Although premontane moist forests of the Central Plateau are largely gone, extensive plantings of shrubs, flowers, and fruiting and flowering trees throughout the San José area have made it ideal for adaptable wildlife species. Shade coffee plantations are preferred habitats for songbirds, including Neotropical migrants. Living fence posts of *Erythrina* and *Tabebuia* are excellent sources of nectar for birds and butterflies. Private gardens abound with butterflies and Rufous-tailed Hummingbirds. Remaining natural places, like the grounds of the Parque Bolívar Zoo in San José, host many wild, free-living butterflies and songbirds.

Caribbean Lowlands

The Caribbean lowlands include moist and wet lowland forests from the Caribbean coast westward to the foothills of Costa Rica's mountains. The Caribbean lowland fauna extends from the Río Frio and Los Chiles area southeastward to Cahuita and the Panama border. For the purposes of this book, the region extends from sea level to the upper limit of the tropical zone at about 2,000 feet elevation. The premontane forest, at least up to about 3,200 feet, also contains many lowland species. This region receives 80 to 200 inches of rainfall annually.

The trees grow to a height of over 150 feet. This is an evergreen forest that receives precipitation throughout the year and does not have a pronounced dry season like the moist and wet forests of the southern Pacific lowlands. Trees include coconut palms (*Cocos*), raffia palms (*Raphia*), *Carapa, Pentaclethra,* kapok (*Ceiba*), swamp almond (*Dipteryx panamensis*), *Alchornea,* walking palm (*Socratea*), and *Pterocarpus*. Tree branches have many epiphytes, such as bromeliads, philodendrons, and orchids. The complexity of the forest canopy contributes to a high diversity of plant and animal species in the treetops. Plants of the understory and forest edge include passionflower (*Passiflora*), *Hamelia, Heliconia,* palms, *Costus,* and *Canna.*

Much of this region has been cleared and settled for production of cattle and bananas. Remaining forest reserves include Tortuguero and Cahuita NPs, Gandoca-Manzanillo NWR, Hitoy-Cerere BR, lower elevations of La Amistad and Braulio Carrillo NPs, and Caño Negro NWR. Tortuguero NP is one of the most extensive reserves and one of the best

Caribbean lowland wet forest, Tortuguero National Park.

remaining examples of rainforest in Central America. Canals at Tortuguero and open water of the Río Frío and at Caño Negro provide excellent opportunities for viewing wildlife from boats. The grounds of Rara Avis also provide an excellent protected reserve at the upper elevational limit of this biological zone. La Selva Biological Field Station, owned and managed by the OTS, has an exceptional boardwalk and trail system that allows easy viewing of rainforests and rainforest wildlife.

Lower levels of Braulio Carrillo NP offer excellent examples of moist and wet lowland forest.

The Caribbean lowlands are significant as an excellent example of tropical habitat that supports classic rainforest species in all their complex diversity, beauty, and abundance.

Highlands

The highland biological zone comprises Costa Rica's four mountain ranges. This zone includes lower montane, montane, and subalpine elevations generally above 4,200 to 4,500 feet in elevation.

Five volcanoes near the Nicaragua border form the Cordillera of Guanacaste: Orosí, Rincón de la Vieja, Santa María, Miravalles, and Tenorio.

The second group of mountains is the Cordillera of Tilarán. It includes the still-active Arenal volcano, which exploded in 1968, and mountains that are part of the Monteverde Cloud Forest.

Third is the Central Cordillera, which includes three large volcanoes that encircle the Central Plateau—Poás, Irazú, and Barva—and Volcano Turrialba southeast of Barva. Poás is active, and Irazú last erupted in 1963. Turrialba was becoming restless in 2008.

The fourth highland region is composed of the great chain of mountains from Cartago to the Panama border. They are the Talamanca Mountains and Cerro de la Muerte, which are of tectonic origin rather than volcanic. Included is Cerro Chirripó, the highest point in Costa Rica at 15,526 feet. These mountains were formed when the Cocos Tectonic Plate pushed up from beneath the ocean onto the Caribbean Tectonic Plate about three to four million years ago. Much of this mountain range is protected as Tapantí NP (11,650 acres), Chirripó NP (123,921 acres), and La Amistad Costa Rica–Panama International Park (479,199 acres).

Crater of Poás volcano.

Talamanca Mountains, Cerro de la Muerte.

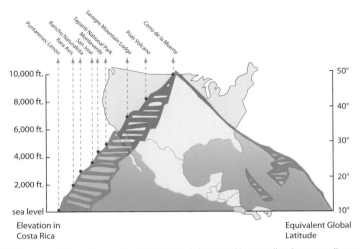

Figure 9. Humboldt's Law: Each 300 feet of ascent on a tropical mountain is comparable to traveling sixty-seven miles north in latitude in terms of changes in average annual temperature.

SPECIES DIVERSITY

Species diversity decreases with increasing elevation. Out of Costa Rica's 882 species of birds, about 130 species can be expected above 6,000 feet. About 105 species can be expected above 7,000 feet, about 85 can be found above 8,000 feet, and about 70 bird species can be expected above 9,000 feet. Comparable trends of lower diversity at higher elevations could also be expected among Costa Rica's invertebrate populations.

HUMBOLDT'S LAW

The South American explorer Alexander von Humboldt recognized an interesting relationship in tropical countries with high mountains. As one travels up a mountain, the average annual temperature decreases by 1 degree Fahrenheit for each increase of 300 feet in elevation. As one travels northward from the equator, the mean annual temperature decreases by

1 degree Fahrenheit for each sixty-seven miles of change in latitude. So an increase of 300 feet elevation on a mountain in the tropics is broadly comparable to traveling sixty-seven miles north. This relationship is portrayed in Figure 9 and is referred to as Humboldt's Law.

Some interesting changes in plant and animal life become apparent in travel up a mountain in the tropics that biologically resemble northward travel in latitude. The relationship of latitude and elevation becomes apparent at higher elevations because there are many temperate-origin plants and birds in the highlands. For example, the avifauna present at 8,000 feet on Costa Rica's mountains includes a higher proportion of temperate-origin thrushes, finches, juncos, and sparrows than is found in the tropical lowlands. It is interesting that the Painted Lady butterfly (*Vanessa virginiensis*) is found in temperate regions of North America and also at the highest elevations in the paramo of Costa Rica.

Figure 10. Costa Rica's five elevational zones.

Many plants of higher elevations in Costa Rica are in the same genera as plants found in the northern United States and Canada, including alders (*Alnus*), oaks (*Quercus*), blueberries (*Vaccinium*), blackberries (*Rubus*), bayberries (*Myrica*), dogwoods (*Cornus*), bearberry (*Arctostaphylos*), Indian paintbrush (*Castilleja*), and boneset (*Eupatorium*). Of course, in temperate areas there is a great deal more variation above and below the annual average temperature than in tropical areas, where there is little variation throughout the year; and in Costa Rica, there has never been a snowfall.

ELEVATIONAL ZONES

To understand the role that elevation plays in plant and animal distribution, it is useful to understand the main categories by which biologists classify elevations and how those zones relate to the highlands. These elevational zones are shown in Figure 10 and described below.

TROPICAL LOWLANDS: The tropical lowland zone ranges from sea level to about 2,300 feet on the Pacific slope and 2,000 feet on the Caribbean slope. The lowland zone includes dry forests like those in Guanacaste as well as moist and wet forests of the southern Pacific and Caribbean lowlands.

PREMONTANE ZONE: This zone is called the "foothills" or "subtropical" zone and is also referred to as the "middle-elevation" zone. Some birds and other animals are found only in the foothills. Examples are Speckled and Silver-throated Tanagers. This zone ranges from about 2,300 feet to 4,900 feet on the Pacific slope and 2,000 feet to 4,600 feet on the Caribbean slope. It could also be called the coffee zone because it is the zone in which the conditions are ideal for coffee production—and for human settlement.

LOWER MONTANE ZONE: The lower montane zone is part of the highlands. It includes the region from 4,900 feet to 8,500 feet on the Pacific slope and 4,600 feet to 8,200 feet on the Caribbean slope. One special habitat that occurs within this zone, and in upper levels of the premontane zone, is cloud forest. The cloud forest occurs roughly from 4,500 to 5,500 feet. A cloud forest, like that at Monteverde, is characterized by fog, mist, and high humidity as well as high precipitation—about 120 to 160 inches per year. The emerging problem of climate change is now causing the Monteverde forests to become drier and is placing cloud forest species of plants and wildlife in serious jeopardy.

Orchids, bromeliads, philodendrons, and dozens of other epiphytes grow in lush profusion among the branches of cloud forest trees.

MONTANE ZONE: The montane zone ranges from 8,500 feet to 10,800 feet on the Pacific slope and from 8,200 feet to 10,500 feet on the Caribbean slope. Among plants of lower montane and montane zones are many of northern temperate origins: oak (*Quercus*), blueberry (*Vaccinium*), bearberry (*Arctostaphylos*), bamboo (*Chusquea*), alder (*Alnus*), bayberry (*Myrica*), magnolia (*Magnolia*), butterfly bush (*Buddleja*), elm (*Ulmus*), mistletoe (*Gaiadendron*), boneset (*Eupatorium*), dogwood (*Cornus*), Indian paintbrush (*Castilleja*), and members of the blueberry family (Ericaceae) like *Satyria, Cavendishia,* and *Psammisia.* Other conspicuous plants are *Oreopanax, Senecio, Miconia, Clusia, Bomarea,* giant thistle (*Cirsium*), *Monochaetum,* wild avocado (*Persea*), poor-man's umbrella (*Gunnera*), and tree ferns.

SUBALPINE PARAMO: Above the montane zone is the area above the treeline called the paramo. It has short, stunted, shrubby vegetation, including bamboo (*Chusquea*), many composites (like *Senecio*), and plants of South American origin from the Andes: a terrestrial bromeliad called *Puya dasylirioides* and a yellow-flowered composite with fuzzy white leaves called lamb's ears (*Espeletia*).

Subalpine rainforest paramo.

Montane wet forest, Cerro de la Muerte.

Cloud forest vegetation, Monteverde.

Coastal Beaches, Islands, and Mangrove Lagoons

The sixth biological zone, not portrayed on the map of biological regions (Fig. 8), includes all Pacific and Caribbean coastlines that extend from Nicaragua to Panama. This shoreline habitat consists of the beaches to the high-tide line and adjacent forests, offshore islands, rocky tidepools exposed at low tide, coral reefs, and mangrove lagoons. Among the more notable islands are Caño Island and Cocos Island. The only coral reef is at Cahuita NP.

Coastal beaches and river estuaries are extremely important as habitat for migratory shorebirds, seabirds, sea turtles, and mangrove-dependent wildlife species. Costa Rica's beaches are extremely important as nesting sites for Green Turtles on the Caribbean coast and for Ridley Turtles, Hawksbill Turtles, and Leatherback Turtles on the Pacific coast.

Other important coastal habitats that are critically endangered by foreign beachfront developers and pollution are those of the mangrove lagoons and mangrove forests. These are important nurseries for fish and wildlife. Significant mangrove lagoons exist at Tamarindo, Playas del Coco, Gulf of Nicoya, Parrita, Golfito, Chomes, Boca Barranca, Quepos, and the 54,362-acre Mangrove Forest Reserve of the Ríos Térraba and Sierpe. They provide exceptional wildlife-watching opportunities during guided boat tours.

WILDLIFE OVERVIEW AND SPECIES COVERAGE

The fauna of Costa Rica includes thousands of birds, mammals, reptiles, amphibians, butterflies, moths, and other invertebrates. This diversity can be both overwhelming and inspiring to a nature enthusiast. Even the casual tourist is drawn to the tropical beauty and appeal of monkeys, motmots, and morphos.

This book has been written to help visitors to Costa Rica know more about the identity and ecology of both common and unusual butterflies, moths, and other

Río Tárcoles estuary.

invertebrates that they may encounter. There are field guides just for birds, reptiles, mammals, or butterflies, but most tourists are interested in all kinds of wildlife. The first edition of the *Field Guide to the Wildlife of Costa Rica*, published in 2002, proved to be very popular. This newly revised approach has split the previous book's wildlife coverage into three volumes. The first covers the country's diverse birdlife, including more than three hundred species accounts. It will leave you overwhelmed by the beauty, diversity, and fascinating ecological adaptations of birds in Costa Rica.

This volume is the second in the series, including more than 100 of the more common and conspicuous butterflies, moths, and other selected invertebrates. Even with that many accounts, this is still just a sampler of the wonderful diversity of Costa Rica's invertebrates. The invertebrates chosen are among the most interesting to tourists, based on my experience in leading tours to Costa Rica since 1987. Some of these are the larger, more colorful species, like morpho butterflies, saturnid moths,

huge beetles, and well-known rainforest insects like army ants.

More than 160 photos, mostly by the author, illustrate the accounts. These photos represent the best photos available from a personal collection of more than 60,000 Costa Rican and Latin American nature and wildlife images. Additional photos have been provided by Dr. Daniel H. Janzen for the *Oxytenis modestia* caterpillar and *Fulgora laternaria*. The postures, behavior, and natural colors displayed by these photos of the creatures alive and in the wild provide the best reference for nature enthusiasts. Paintings usually fail to capture the correct colors, stunning iridescence, and resting postures of many tropical butterflies and other insects, because they are often painted from dead or faded museum specimens.

Most of the author's butterfly photos were taken with a Pentax pz-1 equipped with a Tamron 90 mm macro lens and a 1.7× Pentax teleconverter and a Pentax AF240FT flash. Fuji 100 Sensia I and Sensia II film was used for the slides. Photos

Mangrove lagoon at Quepos.

taken after 2005 were taken with a Canon
20D digital camera.

Over 80 percent of the wildlife images
included in this book were photographed
in the wild, primarily in Costa Rica. Some
have been photographed in the wild in
other countries of Latin America. The
remaining images were taken in captive
settings either in Latin America or the
United States. In only a few cases were
photos of dead specimens used to highlight identification details, like the paired
eyespots on the underside of a Caligo
butterfly's wings. Some photos have been
enhanced through the use of Adobe Pho-
toshop to highlight identification marks
and remove distracting background
features.

BIBLIOGRAPHY

Acuña, Vilma Obando. 2002. Biodiversidad en
Costa Rica. San José, Costa Rica: Editorial
INBIO. 81 pp.
Beletsky, Les. 1998. Costa Rica: The Ecotravel-
lers' Wildlife Guide. San Diego, Calif.: Aca-
demic Press. 426 pp.
Boza, Mario A. 1987. Costa Rica National Parks.
San José, Costa Rica: Fundación Neotrópica.
112 pp.
———. 1988. Costa Rica National Parks. San
José, Costa Rica: Fundación Neotrópica.
272 pp.
Cahn, Robert. 1984. An Interview with Alvaro
Ugalde. The Nature Conservancy News
34(1): 8–15.
Carr, Archie, and David Carr. 1983. A Tiny
Country Does Things Right. International
Wildlife 13(5): 18–25.
Chalker, Mary W. 2007. Exploring Costa Rica
2008/9. San José, Costa Rica: Tico Times.
464 pp.
Cornelius, Stephen E. 1986. The Sea Turtles of
Santa Rosa National Park. San José, Costa
Rica: Fundación de Parques Nacionales.
64 pp.

Ehrenfeld, David. 1989. Places. Orion Nature
Quarterly 8(3): 5–7.
Franke, Joseph. 1997. Costa Rica's National
Parks and Preserves: A Visitor's Guide.
Seattle: The Mountaineers. 223 pp.
Gómez, Luis Diego, and Jay M. Savage. 1983.
Searchers on That Rich Coast: Costa Rican
Field Biology, 1400–1980. In Costa Rican
Natural History, ed. Daniel H. Janzen, 1–11.
Chicago: Univ. of Chicago Press. 816 pp.
Henderson, Carrol L. 1969. Fish and Wildlife
Resources of Costa Rica, with Notes on
Human Influences. Master's thesis, Univ. of
Georgia, Athens. 340 pp.
Holdridge, Leslie R. 1967. Life Zone Ecology.
San José, Costa Rica: Tropical Science Cen-
ter. 206 pp.
inicem. 1998. Costa Rica: Datos e Indicadores
Básicos. Costa Rica at a Glance. Miami:
inicem Group. Booklet. 42 pp.
Janzen, Daniel H. 1990. Costa Rica's New
National System of Conserved Wildlands.
Mimeographed report. 15 pp.
———. 1991. How to Save Tropical Biodiversity:
The National Biodiversity Institute of Costa
Rica. American Entomologist 36(3): 159–171.
Kohl, Jon. 1993. No Reserve Is an Island. Wild-
life Conservation 96(5): 74–75.
Lewin, Roger. 1988. Costa Rican Biodiversity.
Science 242: 1637.
Lewis, Thomas A. 1989. Daniel Janzen's Dry
Idea. International Wildlife 19(1): 30–36.
Market Data. 1993. Costa Rica: Datos e Indica-
dores Básicos. Costa Rica at a Glance. San
José, Costa Rica. 36 pp.
McPhaul, John. 1988. Peace, Nature: C. R.
Aims. Tico Times 32(950): 1, 21.
Meza Ocampo, Tobías A. 1988. Areas Silvestres
de Costa Rica. San Pedro, Costa Rica: Alma
Mater. 112 pp.
Murillo, Katiana. 1999. Ten Years Committed to
Biodiversity. Friends in Costa Rica 3: 23–25.
Pariser, Harry S. 1998. Adventure Guide to
Costa Rica. 3rd ed. Edison, N.J.: Hunter.
546 pp.
Pistorius, Robin, and Jeroen van Wijk. 1993.
Biodiversity Prospecting: Commercial-
izing Genetic Resources for Export.

Biotechnology and Development Monitor 15: 12–15.

Pratt, Christine. 1999. Tourism Pioneer Wins Award, Hosts Concorde. Tico Times 43(1507): 4.

Rich, Pat V., and T. H. Rich. 1983. The Central American Dispersal Route: Biotic History and Paleogeography. In Costa Rican Natural History, ed. Daniel H. Janzen, 12–34. Chicago: Univ. of Chicago Press. 816 pp.

Sandlund, Odd Terje. 1991. Costa Rica's inbio: Towards Sustainable Use of Natural Biodiversity. Norsk Institutt for Naturforskning. Notat 007. Trondheim, Norway. Report. 25 pp.

Sekerak, Aaron D. 1996. A Travel and Site Guide to Birds of Costa Rica. Edmonton, Alberta: Lone Pine. 256 pp.

Skutch, Alexander F. 1971. A Naturalist in Costa Rica. Gainesville: University of Florida Press. 378 pp.

———. 1984. Your Birds in Costa Rica. Santa Monica, Calif.: Ibis. Brochure. 8 pp.

Sun, Marjorie. 1988. Costa Rica's Campaign for Conservation. *Science* 239: 1366–1369.

Tangley, Laura. 1990. Cataloging Costa Rica's Diversity. *BioScience* 40(9): 633–636.

Ugalde, Alvaro F., and María Luisa Alfaro. 1992. Financiamiento de la Conservación en los Parques Nacionales y Reservas Biológicas de Costa Rica. Speech presented at the IV Congreso Mundial de Parques Nacionales, Caracas, Venezuela, February. Mimeographed copy. 16 pp.

Zúñiga Vega, Alejandra. 1991. Archivo de riqueza natural. La Nación, Section B, Viva, February 4.

———. 1991. Estudios de los manglares. La Nación, Section B, Viva, February 4.

SPECIES ACCOUNTS

Siproeta stelenes, one of Costa Rica's most common butterflies

BUTTERFLIES

The abundance and diversity of butterflies and moths bring extra life and beauty to Costa Rica's forests and gardens. Butterflies and moths are dependent on tropical plants as caterpillar food, and they are essential to plants because of their role as flower pollinators. The National Biodiversity Institute (INBIO) has estimated that there are 16,000 butterfly and moth species in Costa Rica, of which about 10 to 15 percent are butterflies. Butterflies and moths may be enjoyed during any time of year, but they are most apparent in the rainy season, primarily June and July.

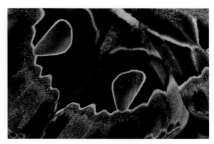

Rothschildia silkmoth, among Costa Rica's largest moths

The beauty of these creatures lies not just in the colors and designs of their wings but also in their amazing adaptations for survival and reproduction. Swallowtail caterpillars mimic bird droppings! Heliconius butterflies warn predators of toxic chemicals in their bodies with bright warning coloration. Caligo butterflies have deceptive eyespots that trick attacking birds. Dozens of butterflies belong to complicated mimicry complexes, in which edible species mimic inedible species that have warning coloration and toxic body chemicals. Some apparent butterflies and wasps are actually moths, and some moths undergo extensive migrations that rival the monarch migrations of North America.

Caligo butterfly wing eyespots

Caterpillars of either butterflies or moths are some of the most beautiful, cryptic, and amazing creatures of the tropical forests. Every caterpillar is adapted in

Morpho helenor wing eyespots

some interesting way to provide protection during that marvelous transition from egg to pupa and then to a flying moth or butterfly. That stage in the life of the insect is filled with threats from creatures ranging from parasitic wasps to assorted birds, reptiles, amphibians, and mammals. The caterpillars cope with this threat with a variety of intriguing adaptations and deceptions. The book *One Hundred Caterpillars* (2006), by J. C. Miller, D. H. Janzen, and W. Hallwachs, provides wonderful details about some of the adaptations and life cycles of Costa Rica's lepidopterans.

Acharia hyperoche, a saddleback caterpillar

Some caterpillars have cryptic camouflage that allows them to be well hidden as they feed on the foliage of their host plant. The *Archeoprepona* butterfly, for example, resorts to marvelous camouflage. The early caterpillar instar larvae appear to be bits of dead leaves. The larger, older caterpillars appear to be a curled up dead leaf draped over a twig. The caterpillar even moves slightly to give the appearance of a leaf moving in the wind.

Some tropical fuzzy caterpillars have urticating hairs that can deliver painful stings to anyone, or any predator, that would touch or grab them. For example, caterpillars in the moth family Limacodidae are referred to as saddleback caterpillars. They are often brightly colored as a form of warning and have venomous spines that deliver severe injuries to any predator or human who touches them.

Learning about these adaptations can add immeasurably to the enjoyment of a nature tour in Costa Rica, as one admires the tropical moths and butterflies, identifies them, and observes their fascinating life histories in person. Don't limit your observations to daytime. Although most butterflies are active in the morning and early afternoon, Caligo butterflies are most active at dawn and dusk. Some tropical lodges like Rancho Naturalista and the Wilson Botanical Garden set up black lights and sheets to attract moths and other insects at night so you can see and marvel at their beauty and adaptations. Other rainforest lodges have security lights at night that also attract nocturnal insects.

The following accounts describe fifty-seven butterflies and twenty-four moths. This is only a sampler of the species in Costa Rica, a small representation of the thousands of species there, but it includes some of the more abundant or conspicuous species that may be encountered while traveling in that country, especially in January and February, the high season when most tourists are visiting Costa Rica. Some species are of particular interest because of their life history or unique adaptations for

Archeoprepona demophoon

survival. Each species account is preceded by the common name (if any), scientific name, Costa Rican name (if any), wing-spread, geographic range, and elevational range. (Many butterflies and moths are referred to only by their scientific names.) For additional details on the butterflies, see volumes 1 and 2 of *The Butterflies of Costa Rica and Their Natural History* (1987 and 1997), by Philip J. DeVries; *Costa Rican Natural History* (1983), edited by Daniel H. Janzen; and *Butterflies and Moths of Costa Rica* (2007), by Isidro Chacón and José Montero. To view photos of Costa Rican caterpillars, see http://janzen.sas.upenn.edu. The distribution maps in these accounts are created largely from sightings made during our Henderson Birding Tours, from the archives of INBIO in Costa Rica, with the institute's permission, and from DeVries (1997). (See Appendix B for details of individual locations and contact information for nearby lodges.) The author wishes to express his sincere appreciation to Dr. Daniel H. Janzen and to INBIO director general Dr. Rodrigo Gámez Lobo and the staff of INBIO for their suggestions regarding the following accounts and for granting me permission to adapt their data and range maps for use in this book.

Much of the most current information on Costa Rica's invertebrates is available on

The butterfly collection of the National Biodiversity Institute, which estimates that there are 16,000 species of butterflies and moths in Costa Rica

the Web at several locations. The best sites include Dr. Janzen's site noted above, which has extensive information on host plants and photos of the species collected in the course of his work. The book *One Hundred Caterpillars*, by Miller, Janzen, and Hallwachs (2006), is highly recommended and is especially useful in learning about the wonderful and complex world of Costa Rican lepidopterans and about the impressive progress that has been made in unraveling the mysteries of butterfly and moth taxonomy in the Guanacaste Conservation Area. Those breakthroughs are attributed to new genetic research in DNA barcoding host plant analysis. On the INBIO site, www .inbio.ac.cr, go to the category "Biodiversidad," and from there to "Biodiversidad en Costa Rica." Click on "Búsqueda de espécimenes" (specimen search) and then on "Informes básicos" (basic information). Type in the name of the species you wish to learn about and specify the type of information you are searching for among INBIO's collection data. Other Web information on butterflies and moths can be found at www.zipcodezoo.com.

José Montero and Isidro Chacón, two of INBIO's preeminent Lepidoptera specialists

SWALLOWTAIL FAMILY *(Papilionidae)*

THOAS SWALLOWTAIL

Heraclides thoas autocles
(formerly Heraclides thoas,
formerly Papilio thoas)
Wingspread: 4.5–4.8 inches.
Range: Nicaragua to Brazil.
Elevational range: Sea level to
3,900 feet.

The Thoas Swallowtail is a large butterfly that is conspicuous as it flies through tropical forests. It is often confused with *Heraclides cresphontes*, but that species has only three yellow spots near the outer margin of the forewing, where *H. t. autocles* has four. This butterfly is most common in moist and wet forests of the Caribbean lowlands and on the southern Pacific slope, but it may also be seen in Guanacaste. Habitat includes forest edges, clearings, or areas along streams where sunlight penetrates the forest canopy.

Adults are fast fliers and are adept at avoiding predation by birds. Among flowers visited for nectar are *Stachytarpheta* and *Lantana*. Males visit wet sand to sip the moisture for salt, which is incorporated into the sperm packet. Apparently females evaluate the salt concentration in a sperm packet before deciding to use the sperm or to digest it. Host plants include *Piper* species and other members of the piper family. Eggs are laid singly and hatch into caterpillars that look like bird droppings! This is a very effective camouflage that discourages birds from eating them.

Thoas Swallowtail caterpillar, a feces mimic

Thoas Swallowtail adult

COSTA RICAN BLACK SWALLOWTAIL

This attractive subspecies of the Black Swallowtail is found at middle to upper elevations of Costa Rica in open areas that have been deforested and converted to meadows or pastures. A sun-loving butterfly, it can be found visiting flowers for nectar during sunny mornings and early afternoons. Host plants include *Apium leptophyllum* and *Foeniculum vulgare*.

Males maintain territories that they defend from other males of the species. DeVries (1987) listed this species as occurring up to an elevation of 5,800 feet, but the individual pictured here was photographed at Savegre Mountain Lodge, at approximately 7,400 feet. This may suggest that the elevational range of some species is moving upward on the mountains as climate change causes warming temperatures at higher elevations.

Papilio polyxenes stabilis
Wingspread: 2.6–2.8 inches.
Range: *P. polyxenes,* Canada to South America; subspecies, Costa Rica to Panama.
Elevational range: 2,700–7,800 feet.

Costa Rican Black Swallowtail

SUBFAMILY RIODININAE

Emesis aurimna (formerly Emesis lucinda aurimna)
Wingspread: 1.9–2.0 inches.
Range: Mexico to Brazil.
Elevational range: Sea level to 5,100 feet.

EMESIS AURIMNA

This is a butterfly of moist and wet lowland and premontane forests on both the Caribbean and Pacific slopes. It occurs at forest and stream edges and openings, where sunlight enhances the growth of flowers that this species uses as nectar sources. The specimen shown here is a female photographed at La Selva Biological Field Station near Puerto Viejo en Sarapiquí. It is medium gray with fine black barring and prominent white spots on the forewings. The male is gray with fine black barring and frosted white tips on the forewings.

Caterpillars eat the foliage of plants in the family Nyctaginaceae, including *Neea laetevirens* and *N. amplifolia*. Adults feed on the nectar of *Croton*, *Hamelia*, *Casearia*, and *Lantana*.

Emesis aurimna female

SUBFAMILY HELICONIINAE

BANDED ORANGE HELICONIAN

As the sole member of its genus, the Banded Orange Heliconian differs from most other Heliconius butterflies in that its orange wings are shorter and broader.

The host plant for the caterpillar is a native passionflower called *Passiflora talamancensis,* as well as other *Passiflora* species. Adults may be seen feeding on the nectar of the tropical milkweed called *Asclepias curassavica.* The Banded Orange Heliconian is uncommon, found in the lowland and premontane elevations of both slopes. As with other members of the subfamily Heliconiae, the bright orange color of the wings serves as a warning to birds.

Dryadula phaetusa
Wingspread: 3.1–3.2 inches.
Range: Mexico to Brazil.
Elevational range: Sea level to 4,800 feet.

Banded Orange Heliconian, dorsal view

Banded Orange Heliconian, side view

JUNO SILVERSPOT

Dione juno
Wingspread: 2.7–3.1 inches.
Range: Central to South America and the Greater Antilles islands.
Elevational range: Sea level to 7,200 feet.

The Juno Silverspot resembles another passionflower butterfly, *Dryas iulia*. The wings are bright orange, but the black edging is more pronounced than on the Julia Butterfly, and the posterior edge of each forewing is jagged. This butterfly is less common than *Dryas iulia*, and the wingspread is slightly smaller. Habitat includes open and disturbed areas, forest edges, and trail sides. It also inhabits the canopy of primary rainforest. This butterfly can be found throughout the year, but it is most abundant during the rainy season. As with *Dryas iulia*, host plants for the caterpillars include members of the genus *Passiflora* in the family Passifloraceae and *Erblichia* in the family Turneraceae.

Juno Silverspot

Juno Silverspot caterpillars

MEXICAN SILVER-SPOTTED FRITILLARY

This bright orange butterfly with silvery markings on the undersurface of the wings gives the appearance of a fritillary. Most North American fritillaries, however, are in the tribe Argynnini. This butterfly is a member of the Heliconid family, which is extremely widespread from the lowlands to over 8,000 feet. It can be found along trails and in open, sunny areas in habitats ranging from natural rainforests to recently deforested lands.

The caterpillars feed on leaves of *Passiflora adenopoda*, *P. capsularis*, and *Tetrastylis lobata*. The adults feed on nectar from a wide variety of flowers, and males may feed on moisture at mud puddles. The butterfly shown here was photographed at an elevation of about 7,500 feet at Savegre Mountain Lodge in the San Gerardo de Dota Valley.

Dione moneta poeyii
Wingspread: 2.9–3.1 inches.
Range: Southern United States through South America.
Elevational range: 3,600–8,400 feet.

Mexican Silver-spotted Fritillary

JULIA BUTTERFLY (ORANGE LONGWING)

Dryas iulia
Wingspread: 3.0–5.6 inches.
Range: Southern Texas and Florida to Brazil.
Elevational range: Sea level to 7,800 feet.

The bright orange Julia Butterfly is one of the most common and easily identified butterflies in the American tropics. Its elongated orange wings with black highlights distinguish it from other passionflower butterflies. The male is bright orange with a slender black marking along the leading edge of the forewing. The female is dull orange with more black edging on the forewing. A species of disturbed areas, forest edges, and forest canopy, the Julia Butterfly is often observed in openings along forest roads and trails where passionflowers (*Passiflora*) occur.

Adults visit many flowers for nectar, including *Lantana*. The host plants on which eggs are laid are limited to the genus *Passiflora*. The Julia Butterfly also visits mud puddles and sandy, wet stream edges to sip mineral-laden moisture. This butterfly is found in the lowlands of both the Pacific and Caribbean slopes. Though usually seen near the ground, it also flies in the forest canopy. Individuals of this butterfly species live only a few weeks.

Julia butterfly female

ISABELLA TIGER

Eueides isabella demonstrates the classic markings of the passionflower butterflies, with orange and black tiger stripes and yellow highlights. These colors serve as a warning to birds that they will get very sick if they eat these brightly colored butterflies. Since many species in this family have similar markings, they are considered members of a mimicry complex.

The host plants for *E. isabella* include the passionflowers *Passiflora platyloba* and *P. ambigua*. One distinguishing mark of the adult is a row of small white dots along the upper side of the trailing edge of the hindwing. The short antennae are usually black on males and yellow on females.

Preferred habitats include mature and second-growth forests, forest edges, gardens, and cleared areas, where they visit a wide variety of flowers at ground level as well as those of trees and vines in the canopy. This species is fairly common in the lowland and premontane levels of both slopes.

Eueides isabella eva
Wingspread: 2.9–3.2 inches.
Range: Mexico to Brazil, and the West Indies.
Elevational range: Sea level to 7,800 feet.

Isabella Tiger

EUEIDES LINEATA

Eueides lineata
Wingspread: 2.4–2.8 inches.
Range: Mexico to Panama.
Elevational range: 1,200–3,300 feet.

This passionflower butterfly is similar to other tiger-striped *Heliconius* and *Eueides* butterflies belonging to a larger complex of Müllerian mimics. They all bear bright orange warning colors and contain powerful cyanogenic glycosides that the caterpillars derive from their passion-flower host plants, in this case, *Passiflora microstipula*. The chemicals can make bird predators very sick if they eat these butterflies. The birds associate the bright orange color with toxic butterflies, making the color an effective deterrent against avian predation. This is one of the small-est passionflower butterflies, and it is also distinguished by the black posterior margin of the hindwing and the black bar through the center of the orange forewing.

The preferred habitat of this rare butterfly includes middle elevation cloud forests, where it can be encoun-tered along the edges of forest openings and roads.

Eueides lineata

HELICONIUS ISMENIUS CLARESCENS

This regionally endemic subspecies of the *Heliconius* genus is found in moist and wet lowland and premontane forests of southwestern Costa Rica. It is rarely found in Guanacaste. Preferred habitats are openings along trails and in light gaps of primary forests, and the period of greatest feeding activity is from morning to mid-afternoon.

Host plants include *Passiflora alata*, *P. pedata*, *P. ambigua*, and *P. platyloba*. Among the flowers visited by *Heliconius ismenius* are species of *Psiguria* and *Gurania*. This is one of the passionflower butterflies that collects pollen on its proboscis and digests it along with the nectar. If you look carefully as it feeds on a flower, you can watch the small blob of pollen accumulate as it feeds. This pollen is a nutritious source of food that extends the life of the butterfly. One place to look for this butterfly is along the trails at Carara NP.

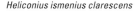

Heliconius ismenius clarescens
Wingspread: 2.9–3.7 inches.
Range: *H. ismenius,* Mexico to Ecuador; subspecies endemic to Costa Rica and Panama.
Elevational range: Sea level to 3,300 feet.

Heliconius ismenius clarescens

HELICONIUS HECALE ZULEIKA

Heliconius hecale zuleika
Wingspread: 3.3–3.9 inches.
Range: Nicaragua to Panama.
Elevational range: Sea level to
4,800 feet.

This is one of the most common of the classic black, orange, and yellow passionflower butterflies in Costa Rica. It is found at lower and middle elevations on both Caribbean and Pacific slopes. As with other Heliconius butterflies, the bright colors are a warning to birds that they contain toxic chemicals that will make them sick if eaten.

They contain cyanogenic glycosides—a cyanide poison that the caterpillars manufacture from passionflower leaves. Other insects cannot eat passionflower leaves, but Heliconius butterflies have the ability to process these poisons. Birds exposed to such toxins respond by retching, vomiting, wiping the bill, fluffing and flattening the feathers, and exhibiting a sickly composure.

This butterfly lays eggs on passionflowers, including *Passiflora vitifolia*, *P. platyloba*, *P. oerstedii*, *P. filipes*, and *P. auriculata*. Adults feed on the nectar of *Psiguria*, *Gurania*, *Lantana*, *Psychotria*, *Hamelia*, and *Anguria*. In addition to feeding on nectar, this butterfly collects pollen on its proboscis. It makes a slurry in the rolled proboscis. Amino acids leach into the nectar, and this is swallowed by the butterfly. The high protein content of the amino acids from the pollen gives this butterfly an increased life span and greater reproductive potential. Although most butterflies live only about ten days, individuals of this species may live up to nine months.

Heliconius hecale zuleika

ZEBRA LONGWING

The Zebra Longwing is one of fourteen *Heliconius* butterflies in Costa Rica. It is a species of open areas, pastures, gardens, forest edges, coffee plantations, and roadside ditches. The genus is well known for its host-plant relationships to passionflowers and its fascinating mimicry patterns. This species is the only member of the genus with a pattern of yellow stripes and spots on a black background.

Adults visit *Lantana, Stachytarpheta, Cissus, Rytidostylis,* and *Hamelia.* This butterfly gathers pollen on its proboscis, as do *Heliconius hecale zuleika* and *H. erato.* The improved nutrition from the pollen helps them live up to three months and allows females to lay up to 1,000 eggs. Without pollen, they may live only a month. Adults roost in groups of up to seventy individuals at night.

The caterpillars have some incredible adaptations. They feed on *Passiflora* leaves that are toxic or deadly to other butterflies of this genus, including *P. lobata, P. biflora, P. menispermifolia, P. adenopoda,* and *P. pulchella.* This is the only caterpillar that can feed on leaves of the plant *Tetrastylis.* Adult male Zebra Longwings have one other unusual habit. They mate with the female before she emerges from her chrysalis. The Zebra Longwing is found on both slopes at lower and middle elevations but is less common in the southern Pacific region and at high elevations.

Heliconius charithonia charithonia
Costa Rican name: *Zebra; zebrita.*
Wingspread: 3.0–3.5 inches.
Range: Southern Texas and Florida to Peru.
Elevational range: Sea level to 7,800 feet.

Zebra Longwing

Small Postman showing pollen slurry on proboscis

SMALL POSTMAN

Heliconius erato petiverana is the most common *Heliconius* butterfly in Costa Rica. Its black, yellow, and red pattern is conspicuous as it visits flowers of disturbed forest edges, second-growth forests, roadsides, coffee plantations, and gardens. Occurring on both Pacific and Caribbean slopes, this butterfly, like other members of its genus, is long-lived because it feeds on pollen as well as nectar. Adults visit flowers of *Psiguria, Lantana, Psychotria, Cissus, Anguria, Rytidostylis*, and *Hamelia*.

Eggs are laid singly at the tips of passionflower leaves, and host species include *Passiflora talamancensis, P. coriacea, P. costaricensis*, and *P. biflora*. Adults roost in groups of up to ten individuals near the ground in second-growth vegetation.

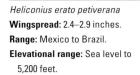

Heliconius erato petiverana
Wingspread: 2.4–2.9 inches.
Range: Mexico to Brazil.
Elevational range: Sea level to
5,200 feet.

Small Postman

POSTMAN

The Postman is one of the classic rainforest butterflies, along with morphos and caligos, that are worth looking for while visiting Costa Rica. They display a striking combination of black, red, and yellow that serves as a warning to birds that might consider eating then. *Heliconius melpomene* is a nearly identical Müllerian mimic of *Heliconius erato*. That means that both species share toxic qualities if eaten, and birds avoid both species since they look alike. This is one of the most incredible mimicry complexes in Latin America. Processes of natural selection have resulted in the development of twelve different color patterns, or subspecies, for *H. erato* throughout its range from Mexico to Brazil. In eleven of the twelve cases, the distinctive color pattern of each *H. erato* subspecies is almost perfectly mimicked by the color patterns of *H. melpomene* in the same area.

The subtle differences in these two butterflies include the yellow stripe on the underside of the hindwing. This stripe extends to the top of the hindwing when the butterfly is at rest with the wings closed in *H. erato*, and it stops short of the upper edge of the hindwing on *H. melpomene*. Also, there are four tiny red spots on the underside of the hindwing where the wing attaches to the thorax on *H. erato* and only three tiny red spots on *H. melpomene*.

This uncommon passionflower butterfly is found in the lowlands and premontane moist and wet forests of both the Caribbean and Pacific lowlands. It occurs along partially shaded trails and forest edges. Host plants include *Passiflora oerstedii* and *P. menispermifolia*. Among the flowers visited for nectar are *Lantana*, *Hamelia*, and *Cissus*. Like *H. erato*, this species collects pollen from plants like *Psiguria* and makes a pollen-nectar slurry, which it consumes.

Heliconius melpomene rosina
Wingspread: 2.8–3.3 inches.
Range: *H. melpomene*, Mexico to Brazil; subspecies, Mexico to Panama.
Elevational range: Sea level to 1,500 feet.

Heliconius melpomene

Postman

Heliconius erato

HELICONIUS CLYSONYMUS MONTANUS

Heliconius clysonymus montanus
Wingspread: 2.8–3.2 inches.
Range: *H. clysonymus,* Honduras to Ecuador; subspecies endemic from Costa Rica to Panama.
Elevational range: 2,400–5,400 feet.

This black, yellow, and red member of the Heliconius mimicry complex is a high-elevation species found from premontane to montane levels in the mountains of Costa Rica. All of the other members are found from lowland to premontane elevations. Like other members of this genus, however, they are most likely to be seen visiting flowers at sunny sites along trails and forest openings.

Host plants for the caterpillars are passionflowers, including *Passiflora apetala* and *P. biflora*. Flowers visited for nectar and pollen include members of the genera *Gurania* and *Psiguria*.

Heliconius clysonymus montanus

HELICONIUS CYDNO GALANTHUS

This boldly marked black, white, and red butterfly is a Müllerian mimicry partner with the similarly marked *Heliconius sapho leuce*. The butterfly is black with bold broad white stripes on each forewing. When the wings are closed, a double circle of red is visible on the underwing. Both it and its mimicry partner are found in primary moist and wet forests of the Caribbean lowlands and premontane forests. Occasionally they are found in secondary forests.

The host plants of the caterpillars are passionflowers, including *Passiflora vitifolia* and *P. biflora*. Adults visit flowers of plants like *Psiguria* for both nectar and pollen, which are ingested as a nutritious slurry that helps the butterflies live longer.

Heliconius cydno galanthus
Wingspread: 2.9–3.3 inches.
Range: *H. cydno,* Mexico to Ecuador; subspecies, Mexico to Costa Rica.
Elevational range: Sea level to 5,100 feet.

Heliconius cydno galanthus

HELICONIUS ELEUCHIA

Heliconius eleuchia
Wingspread: 2.8–3.2 inches.
Range: Costa Rica to Colombia.
Elevational range: 300–2,100 feet.

Heliconius eleuchia is a rare passionflower butterfly found only on the Caribbean slope of Costa Rica in the lower foothills at the upper levels of the lowlands and lower levels of premontane wet forests. The bold black, iridescent blue, and yellow markings appear to make it a mimicry partner with similar members of the genus, like *Heliconius sara*. The white band along the edge of the hindwing is a characteristic of *H. cydno chioneus*. The distribution extends from the northern foothills at La Virgen del Socorro southeastward toward Panama. The preferred habitat appears to be along the edges of rivers.

The host plant is believed to be *Passiflora tica*. Plants visited for nectar include *Psychotria,* which is common in riparian areas. When mating, this species does not wait for the female to emerge from the pupa. He mates with her through the chrysalis before she hatches.

Heliconius eleuchia

HELICONIUS SARA

This butterfly is considered a specialist because only one passionflower species serves as its host plant, *Passiflora auriculata*. *Heliconius sara* shares black, iridescent blue, and yellow markings with other *Heliconius* butterflies, like *Heliconius pachinus*, *H. hewitsoni*, and *H. eleuchia*. There are two subspecies in Costa Rica, *H. s. fulgidus* in the Caribbean rainforest lowlands and *H. s. theudela* in the Pacific moist and wet forests. The main difference is that the trailing edge of the hindwing is black on *H. s. fulgidus* and the trailing edge is yellow on *H. s. theudela*.

Like the Zebra Longwing (*H. charithonia charithonia*), the males of this butterfly will mate with the female while she is still in her chrysalis.

This passionflower butterfly inhabits forest edges and openings mainly in the vicinity of its host plant, *Passiflora auriculata*. Adults visit flowers of *Hamelia*, *Psiguria*, *Lantana*, and *Palicourea* for both nectar and pollen.

Heliconius sara
Wingspread: 1.9–2.4 inches.
Range: Mexico to Brazil.
Elevational range: Sea level to 4,200 feet.

Heliconius sara

LAPARUS DORIS

Laparus doris (formerly Heliconius doris)
Wingspread: 2.8–3.5 inches.
Range: Mexico to Brazil.
Elevational range: Sea level to 3,600 feet.

Until recently, *Laparus doris* was included in the genus *Heliconius,* but it was found to have a different number of chromosomes from the *Heliconius* species. It is an extremely attractive passionflower butterfly, and its variety of sizes and color phases have kept taxonomists intrigued and confused. The hindwings feature a colorful ray pattern of red, green, or blue, and the forewings are black with yellow spots. All color phases can be derived from the same clutch of eggs.

The host plant of *Laparus doris* is the passionflower *Passiflora ambigua. Psiguria* species are among the flowers visited for nectar and for pollen. The pollen helps the butterflies live longer than they would if they fed on nectar alone.

This species is found in forested habitats and is most commonly observed at light gaps along forest edges where flowers are more numerous.

Laparus doris, blue color phase

Laparus doris, red color phase

SUBFAMILY ACRAEINAE

ACTINOTE ANTEAS

Actinote anteas

This small orange, black, and yellow butterfly at first appears to be a distasteful Heliconius butterfly, with markings similar to those of the *Eueides* species and *Heliconius ismenius*. One of its distinguishing marks consists of black veins on the dorsal surface of the orange hindwings. It belongs, however, to an entirely different subfamily of butterflies, called Acraeinae, and its genus is found both in Africa and in the American tropics. A common ancestor likely existed before continental drift split Africa from South America. This genus appears to have developed mimicry complexes in an example of convergent evolution similar to the complex for Heliconius butterflies.

Actinote butterflies have markings similar to members of the Heliconiiae butterflies, so they are able to take advantage of a Müllerian mimicry complex (similar species that are all distasteful to birds) that crosses subfamily boundaries. Their distasteful qualities, however, come not from passionflowers but from host plants in the aster family that contain toxic chemicals known as pyrolizidine alkaloids. When one of these butterflies is grabbed and squeezed, as by a bird, it oozes liquid from its thorax that presumably contains these nasty, distasteful chemicals. The host plants for *Actinote anteas* are species of *Mikania,* a genus in the aster family.

There are also two kinds of similar butterflies (*Castilia* and *Eresia*) that resemble *Actinote anteas* but are not distasteful; they form a Batesian mimicry complex with *Actinote.*

This is a foothill species, found on both Caribbean and Pacific slopes in open, sunny areas like pastures and forest clearings, where they feed on nectar of *Lantana* and *Asclepias* species.

Actinote anteas
Wingspread: 1.9–2.3 inches.
Range: Mexico to Venezuela.
Elevational range: 300–4,500 feet.

Hypanartia dione arcaei

---

*Hypanartia dione arcaei (formerly
Hypanartia arcaei)*
Wingspread: 2.2–2.3 inches.
Range: Costa Rica and Panama.
Elevational range: 3,600–10,200
feet.

SUBFAMILY NYMPHALINAE

HYPANARTIA DIONE ARCAEI

Hypanartia dione arcaei is a medium-sized brown butterfly of higher elevations with a conspicuous orange patch on each forewing and a short tail on each hindwing. This butterfly is usually encountered in Cerro de la Muerte, in the Talamanca Mountains, and in the San Gerardo de Dota region, including Savegre Mountain Lodge, as well as on the Cacao Volcano in the Guanacaste Conservation Area. Host plants for this genus include the nettles *Urera eggersii* and *Myriocarpa longipes* and a member of the Cecropiaceae family, *Cecropia polyphlebia*. Preferred habitats include cloud forests and montane oak forests.

This attractive butterfly is usually solitary and may be found at wet sites like river edges and water seepages. It will also visit the large yellow flowers of *Senecio megaphylla*. At one site in Cerro de la Muerte, this butterfly landed on the binoculars of the author's wife Ethelle and spent several minutes perched there, suggesting that it was attracted to salt concentrations from perspiration deposits.

PAINTED LADY

The Painted Lady is the most widely distributed butterfly in the world. It can be enjoyed in backyard gardens
throughout North America, among paramo flowers in
the Talamanca Mountains, and at high elevations in the
Andes of South America. Although the butterfly is common in temperate latitudes, in Costa Rica its distribution
is limited mainly to the treeless paramo life zone of the
Talamanca Mountains.

The host plants of the Painted Lady include *Cirsium,
Carduus, Centaurea, Arctium*, and *Artemisia*. Giant
thistles (*Cirsium*) over ten feet tall are common at higher
elevations and are likely a commonly used host plant in
Costa Rica. The author has observed these butterflies
feeding on the nectar of a species of *Espeletia,* a yellow
composite called lamb's ears.

Look for the Painted Lady at flowers on the transmission tower site at kilometer 90 on the Pan American
Highway in Cerro de la Muerte. Because of the cool environment in which it lives, it is usually active only during
periods of warmer, sunny weather in the mornings.

*Vanessa virginiensis (formerly
   Vanessa cardui)*
Wingspread: 2.3–2.5 inches.
Range: All continents except
   Antarctica and Australia
   (including the country of New
   Zealand).
Elevational range: 2,700–10,200
   feet.

Painted Lady

GIANT PATCH

Chlosyne janais
Wingspread: 1.7–2.4 inches.
Range: Mexico to Colombia.
Elevational range: Sea level to 3,600 feet.

Chlosyne janais is one of the more common garden butterflies that may be seen in the Central Plateau region. It occurs around San José as well as in lowland and premontane elevations of both the Caribbean and Pacific slopes. Distinguishing marks are scattered small white dots on the black forewing and an orange hindwing with a broad black edge on the male. It is an adaptable species found in sunny gardens, pastures, and deforested habitats where flowers are available in abundance as nectar sources. Host plants include *Odontonema,* a genus in the family Acanthaceae.

Some of the butterflies in this genus are believed to be distasteful because of chemicals they acquire from their host plants as caterpillars, so their conspicuous orange, black, and yellow markings apparently serve as warning coloration in mimicry complexes that have not been as well studied as those of the Heliconius butterflies.

Giant Patch

CHLOSYNE NARVA

In contrast to the widespread and adaptable *Chlosyne janais* species, *Chlosyne narva* is a rainforest species of Costa Rica's lowlands and lower premontane elevations of the Caribbean slope and southern Pacific slope. The author has photographed this butterfly along the Río Madrigal on the Osa Peninsula of southwestern Costa Rica. It is black and orange with white spots along the black margins of the forewings and hindwings.

Its preferred habitat includes sunlit areas in forests along streams, beaches, forest openings, and roads. The flowers visited for nectar include *Lantana*, *Psychotria*, and members of the aster family.

Chlosyne narva bonpland
Wingspread: 2.0–2.7 inches.
Range: Nicaragua to Venezuela.
Elevational range: Sea level to 3,900 feet.

Chlosyne narva

ANTHANASSA ARDYS

Anthanassa ardys
Wingspread: 2.3–2.5 inches.
Range: Southern Mexico to
   Colombia.
Elevational range: 3,000–4,800 feet.

Anthanassa ardys is one of many tropical butterflies that are still poorly understood because their life history and taxonomic relationships have not been adequately delineated. In contrast to many vertebrates that have been well studied, many butterflies continue to challenge biologists and taxonomists because of this lack of adequate natural history research. In the case of *Anthanassa ardys*, the host plant is still unknown and the life history of the caterpillars is unknown. Yet, it is a common butterfly of open areas such as pastures and fields on both the Caribbean and Pacific slopes. Adults show a preference for feeding on the nectar of asters.

Anthanassa ardys

COLOBURA DIRCE

Colobura dirce is a common butterfly of tropical lowland and premontane elevations wherever Cecropia trees are found. Cecropia leaves are the host plant food of the caterpillars, including *C. insignis, C. obtusifolia,* and *C. peltata.* This butterfly is dark on the upper side with a wide, diagonal creamy yellow band across each forewing. The most distinguishing feature, however, is on the underwing. When at rest, it holds its wings together and displays fine black-and-white striping on the underwings.

In contrast to many butterflies that feed on nectar, this butterfly is a real garbage mouth. It is attracted to rotten bananas, mangoes, papayas, and guavas; juices of dead rotting animals; animal feces; and even wet laundry on backyard clotheslines.

Colobura dirce
Wingspread: 2.8–2.9 inches.
Range: Mexico to South America.
Elevational range: Sea level to
4,200 feet.

Colobura dirce

SMYRNA BLOMFILDIA

Smyrna blomfildia
Wingspread: 2.7–3.2 inches.
Range: Mexico to Peru.
Elevational range: Sea level to 5,400 feet.

Like *Colobura dirce*, this species has fine zebra stripes against a white background on its underwings. These show up well when it closes its wings to feed. Another similarity with *Colobura* is that it feeds on the juices of rotten fruits and animal dung.

Host plants are in the nettle family (Urticaceae), including *Urera baccifera, Urera caracasana,* and *Myriocarpa longipes.* Habitat preferences include dry, moist, and wet forests of both the Caribbean and Pacific slopes in the lowlands and at premontane levels. This butterfly feeds at ground level and at lower canopy levels of the forest.

Smyrna blomfildia

MALACHITE

The Malachite is a medium-sized butterfly with green-ish spots and blotches on the dorsal and ventral wing surfaces. One of the most common butterflies in Central America, it lives along forest edges, disturbed second growth, and in rural and urban gardens. This butter-fly is conspicuous on sunny days and occurs on both the Caribbean and Pacific slopes at lower and middle elevations.

In addition to visiting flowers, *Siproeta stelenes* visits rotting fruits, carrion, and bat dung under bat roosts. Adults roost in groups on shrubs close to the ground. Females lay single eggs on new leaves of plants in the Acanthaceae family, including *Ruellia coccinea* and *R. metallica*; *Justicia candalerianae* and *J. cartha-ginensis*; and *Blechum brownei*, *B. blechum*, and *B. pyramidatum*.

Siproeta stelenes
Wingspread: 3.5–3.8 inches.
Range: South Florida and Texas to Brazil.
Elevational range: Sea level to 4,800 feet.

Malachite

SIPROETA EPAPHUS

Siproeta epaphus
Wingspread: 3.4–3.5 inches.
Range: Mexico to Peru.
Elevational range: 2,100–5,400 feet.

This impressive orange, black, and yellow butterfly is a foothill species found in moist and wet forests at premontane levels of both the Caribbean and Pacific slopes. The preferred habitats are sunny forest edges and riverbanks where it can locate its host plants in the family Acanthaceae, such as species of *Ruellia, Justicia, Hygrophila,* and *Blechum.*

Siproeta epaphus feeds on the nectar of flowers characteristic of forest openings, roadsides, and river edges, like *Croton, Lantana,* and *Impatiens.* Males can be seen feeding on moisture from wet sand along riverbanks, and this butterfly will also feed on juices of rotten fruits, carrion, and animal feces.

Siproeta epaphus

BANDED PEACOCK

The Banded Peacock is the most common butterfly in Costa Rica. It is found in meadows; along roadsides, pastures, and riverbanks, and in deforested areas. It occurs in Guanacaste and in Caribbean and southern Pacific regions. It lives from the lowlands to the highlands and at middle elevations like the Wilson Botanical Garden at San Vito and Monteverde. The medium brown to dark brown wings have conspicuous yellow or white bands and red highlights on the hindwings. Newly emerged male butterflies have yellow bands that eventually fade to white. Newly emerged females may have yellow or white bands, but the yellow-banded females also fade to white.

Caterpillars feed primarily on plants in the Acanthaceae family, including *Blechum brownei* and *B. pyramidatum*, found in disturbed places. Other host plants include *Justicia candalerianae*, *Dicliptera unguiculata*, *Hygrophila costata*, and *Ruellia*. This butterfly is active in sunny areas throughout the day and feeds primarily on nectar of second-growth plants like *Lantana*, *Emilia*, and *Cosmos*. An adult may live about two weeks.

Not protected by toxic chemicals in its body, this butterfly is preyed upon by spiders, praying mantises, frogs, lizards, birds, and mammals. Males are so overzealous in defending territories that they pursue not only other males of their species but also other butterfly species, birds, and even humans.

Banded Peacock, older adult with faded white wing bars

Anartia fatima
Costa Rican name: *Cocinera.*
Wingspread: 2.1–2.4 inches.
Range: Mexico to eastern Panama.
Elevational range: Sea level to 9,400 feet.

Banded Peacock, newly hatched with yellow wing bars

WHITE PEACOCK

Anartia jatrophae luteipicta
Wingspread: 2.3–2.4 inches.
Range: Southern United States to South America.
Elevational range: Sea level to 4,500 feet.

At first glance, *Anartia jatrophae* appears to be a variety of the *Hamadryas* cracker butterfly. It belongs to a different genus, however, and has an entirely different lifestyle. This is a common butterfly of tropical lowlands and lower premontane levels of both Caribbean and Pacific slopes in forest openings, deforested areas, pastures, gardens, and roadsides. It is more abundant in moist and wet lowland forests of the southern Pacific coast.

Host plants span four plant genera in three families, providing a wide variety of habitat choices for this species. Host plant species in the family Scrophulariaceae include *Stemodia durantifolia;* in the family Verbenaceae they include *Lippia bracterosa* and *Phyla nodiflora.* Other host plants include species of *Blechum, Ruellia, Bacopa,* and *Lindernia.* This butterfly is active during sunny daylight hours and can be observed at common flowers of *Lantana, Stachytarpheta,* and *Impatiens* species.

White Peacock

SUBFAMILY LIMENITIDINAE

ADELPHA CYTHEREA MARCIA

This common butterfly inhabits disturbed habitats. It is brown with white bands on the hindwings, and it is one of many tropical butterflies that have prominent orange bands on the forewings aligned with continuous white bands on the posterior of the forewings and adjacent hindwings. Inhabiting moist and wet lowlands of the Caribbean and southern Pacific regions, this butterfly is absent from Guanacaste's dry forests. It frequents forest edges, beaches, and forest openings. The host plant, *Sabicea villosa*, belongs to the coffee family (Rubiaceae) and is found in disturbed places. Adults feed on the juices of rotting fruits and the nectar of asters and hot lips (*Cephaelis*). There are thirty species in the genus *Adelpha* in Costa Rica, and they can be difficult to identify.

Adelpha cytherea marcia
Wingspread: 1.8–2.0 inches.
Range: Guatemala to Colombia.
Elevational range: Sea level to 3,600 feet.

Adelpha cytherea marcia

Adelpha iphiclus

Adelpha iphiclus
Wingspread: 2.0–2.3 inches.
Range: Mexico to Brazil.
Elevational range: Sea level to
 2,700 feet.

ADELPHA IPHICLUS

This small brown butterfly has an orange spot on the tip of each forewing and a broad white diagonal band across each forewing and hindwing. It is one of Costa Rica's most commonly observed butterflies. The markings are similar to many other *Adelpha* species. Of the thirty or so species of this genus in Costa Rica, most have a brown background, orange spots, and white wing bars. The conspicuous markings appear to signal a mimicry complex similar to that of the Heliconius butterflies, but the mystery is that apparently all of the *Adelpha* butterflies are edible. They contain no toxic chemicals that would make their bird predators sick. It is neither a Müllerian or a Batesian mimicry complex.

It is possible, however, that *Adelpha iphiclus* and its relatives derive some benefit from their similar markings. It is the author's opinion that the *Adelpha* butterflies form an edible mimicry complex, in which the attention of predators is diluted among many species with similar markings rather than focused on one particular species with memorable markings. The survival of individuals of a species without chemical defenses is thus increased.

This *Adelpha* species is found on both Caribbean and Pacific slopes, but it is more abundant on the Pacific side. It is found in dry, moist, and wet forests and is common in forest openings, roadsides, and gardens. Host plants include species in the family Rubiaceae: *Calycophyllum candidissimum, Randia thurberi, Rustia costaricensis,* and *Uncaria tomentosa.* Adults feed on the nectar of flowers of *Vochysia* and *Paullinia* plants and on juices of guava, *Genipa,* mango, and *Guazuma ulmifolia.* They also feed on juices of animal dung.

ADELPHA TRACTA

This is one of the few examples of this genus that does not have an orange spot on each forewing and a white diagonal band across the forewings and hindwings. Instead, it has a brown background with orange stripes along the edge of the forewings and hindwings. It is a species of upper elevations, including the premontane, lower montane, and lower levels of montane forests on both slopes.

Preferred habitats include sunny openings along roads, trails, and forest openings. These butterflies can often be found resting on the ground or on vegetation near ground level until temperatures warm up in the afternoon.

The host plants include two species in the family Caprifoliaceae, *Viburnum costaricanum* and *V. venustum*. Foods of adults include rotten fruits of melastomes, fruits of the laurel (avocado) family, and mammal dung. Males feed on moisture derived from wet sand.

Adelpha tracta
Wingspread: 2.1–2.5 inches.
Range: Costa Rica and Panama.
Elevational range: 2,700–7,500 feet.

Adelpha tracta

SUBFAMILY APATURINAE

Doxocopa laure
Wingspread: 2.4–2.6 inches.
Range: Mexico to Brazil.
Elevational range: Sea level to 3,000 feet.

SILVER EMPEROR

Doxocopa laure is similar to *Adelpha cytherea*, in that it is brown with white bands through the wings and orange on the forward portion of each white band. This coloration would appear to be an example of mimicry, but since these butterflies do not contain toxic chemicals that deter predators, the reason for the resemblance is unknown. As suggested in the account for *Adelpha iphiclus*, perhaps this species is part of an edible mimicry complex, in which the attention of bird predators is dispersed among many species, minimizing the cumulative predatory impact on any one species. The male has iridescent purple and blue highlights adjacent to the white bands. Host plants are trees and shrubs in the elm family (Ulmaceae), including *Celtis iguanaea*.

    Doxocopa laure occurs on the Pacific and Caribbean slopes, including Guanacaste's dry forests. Adults visit *Croton* and *Cordia* flowers as well as wet sand containing animal urine and fresh mammal droppings. Among locations where this butterfly can be seen are Santa Rosa NP and Monteverde.

Silver Emperor female

TURQUOISE EMPEROR

The male of this small rainforest butterfly has an iridescent turquoise band across the dorsal surface of the wings.
A middle-elevation species of forests in the foothills of
both the Caribbean and Pacific slopes, its host plant is
unknown. The males appear to defend feeding territories
in sunny edges of the forest understory, where they may
perch on vegetation or on wet sand. They will chase away
other butterflies that come into their territories. Females,
which lack the turquoise iridescence of the males, feed on
rotting fruit on the ground. Females have a longitudinal
whitish stripe on each side of the body on the dorsal side
of the wings, with soft blue accents on the white of the
hindwing.

Doxocopa cherubina (formerly
Doxocopa laurentina cherubina)
Wingspread: 2.4–2.9 inches.
Range: Mexico to Colombia.
Elevational range: 300–5,100 feet.

Turquoise Emperor male

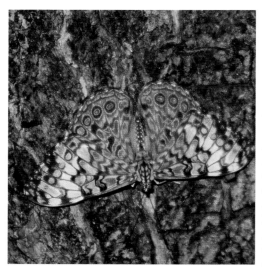

Guatemalan Cracker

Hamadryas guatemalena
  guatemalena
Costa Rican names: *Calicó;*
  soñadora común.
Wingspread: 2.75–3.5 inches.
Range: Mexico to Brazil
  (subspecies, Mexico to Costa
  Rica).
Elevational range: Sea level to
  2,100 feet.

SUBFAMILY BIBLIDINAE

GUATEMALAN CRACKER

The camouflage markings of the cracker (or calico) butterflies allow these species to seem to disappear when they land on a tree trunk. They rest upside down and are known for an unusual cracking sound that they make in flight, often as they chase away other butterflies. The sound can be heard up to sixty feet away and was first reported by Charles Darwin when he explored South America. The Guatemalan Cracker is found only on the Pacific slope in dry, moist, and wet forests but is most common in the dry forests of Guanacaste, especially in the rainy season.

There are nine kinds of cracker butterflies in the country. Several have the mottled gray or brownish camouflage markings, including *H. guatemalena, H. februa,* and *H. feronia.* Since they depend on camouflage for survival, they do not have protective chemical defenses in their bodies. They are preyed on by Rufous-tailed Jacamars. Adults do not feed on flower nectar. They sip juices of rotting fruit, fermented sap from leguminous trees, and animal dung. The only host plants on which females lay eggs are species in the euphorbia family, including *Dalechampia scandens, D. cissifolia,* and *D. heteromorpha.*

GRAY CRACKER

The Gray Cracker, the most common cracker butterfly in Costa Rica, is distinguished from the Guatemalan species by red crescents on the tiny eyespots of the hindwing margins. It occurs throughout the country in the lowlands of both slopes but is most common in forests of Guanacaste.

The host plants of this cracker butterfly, like the Guatemalan Cracker, are in the euphorbia family, including *Dalechampia scandens*.

Hamadryas februa ferentina
Costa Rican names: *Calicó; soñadora común.*
Wingspread: 2.6–3.1 inches.
Range: Southern United States to Brazil.
Elevational range: Sea level to 3,900 feet.

Gray Cracker

VARIABLE CRACKER

Hamadryas feronia farinulenta
Costa Rican names: *Calicó;*
soñadora común.
Wingspread: 2.75–3.0 inches.
Range: Southern United States to
Brazil (subspecies endemic to
Central America).
Elevational range: Sea level to
3,000 feet.

Another of the cracker butterflies in Costa Rica is the Variable Cracker. This species is similar to *H. februa,* but it lacks the reddish orange crescents in the ocelli on the hindwings of *H. februa.*

The broad range includes both Caribbean and Pacific slopes and dry, moist, and wet forest habitats. Host plants are in the euphorbia family, including species in the genus *Dalechampia.* This cracker butterfly is less common than the Guatemalan and Gray species.

Variable Cracker

STARRY NIGHT CRACKER

Although *Hamadryas saurites* is in the genus of cracker butterflies, it is black with stunning iridescent blue spots. DeVries (1987) refers to it as the "starry night" hamadryas. Host plants include at least five species in the genus *Dalechampia,* in the family Euphorbiaceae. The caterpillar apparently sequesters bad-tasting toxic chemicals from this plant, because the butterfly is avoided by jacamars. The bright blue highlights serve as a warning coloration.

The distribution includes Caribbean and Pacific slopes to an elevation of about 3,000 feet, but it is most common in the middle and upper canopy of Caribbean lowland forests. While at rest, *H. saurites* perches upside down on tree trunks with the wings open. It feeds on juices of rotting fruits.

Hamadryas saurites (formerly Hamadryas laodamia saurites)
Wingspread: 2.6–2.8 inches.
Range: Mexico to Brazil.
Elevational range: Sea level to 3,000 feet.

Starry Night Cracker male

Starry Night Cracker female

BLUE CRACKER

Hamadryas ariensis (formerly Hamadryas arinome)
Wingspread: 2.5–2.7 inches.
Range: Mexico to Brazil.
Elevational range: Sea level to 2,100 feet.

The Blue Cracker is similar to the Starry Night Cracker, and the females could be confused, but the white bar across the forewing of the *H. saurites* female is fairly straight and more cream-colored. On the forewing of *H. ariensis*, the bar is whiter and has jagged edges. Also, the iridescent spots along the trailing edge of the hindwing are enclosed in elongated oval blue marks that point toward the center of the butterfly.

As a brightly marked butterfly with blue iridescence, this species appears to be part of a Müllerian mimicry complex, in partnership with *H. saurites* and *H. amphinome*. They are all distasteful to butterfly predators like jacamars. This quality is acquired by the caterpillars from feeding on plants in the euphorbia family, including *Dalechampia cissifolia, D. heteromorpha,* and *D. websteri.*

Like other members of this genus, this species perches upside down on tree trunks. Blue Crackers live in tropical moist and wet forests of tropical lowlands on the Caribbean slope; they are seldom encountered because they are believed typically to feed on rotting fruits in the forest canopy.

Blue Cracker female

BERANIA DAGGERWING

Marpesia berania is one of eight daggerwing butterflies in Costa Rica. Common throughout the country, it is characterized by distinctive tails on the hindwing, an orange base color, and slender longitudinal brown bands on the wings. The distribution includes both Caribbean and Pacific lowlands in a wide variety of habitats. It is most common in moist and wet lowland forests and less common in the tropical dry forests of Guanacaste. Adults visit the blossoms of *Cordia* and *Croton* bushes.

Males may gather in large numbers along riverbanks, where they feed on moisture in the sand. *Marpesia berania* sleeps in groups of up to fifty butterflies. This daggerwing lives much longer than many butterflies—up to five months. Host plants are in the family Moraceae, including *Clarisia mexicana* and *Trophis involucrata*.

Marpesia berania
Wingspread: 2.4–2.5 inches.
Range: Mexico through Brazil.
Elevational range: Sea level to 3,300 feet.

Berania Daggerwing

Many-banded Daggerwing

Marpesia chiron
Wingspread: 2.3–2.4 inches.
Range: Southern United States to South America.
Elevational range: Sea level to 900 feet.

MANY-BANDED DAGGERWING

Marpesia daggerwing butterflies look like miniature brown swallowtails. They are typically orange to brownish with a series of longitudinal dark stripes and a pair of tails. The Many-banded Daggerwing is a common and widespread species, found from lowland forests through montane forest elevations. It is more common above 1,500 feet and is most commonly encountered at wet sandy spots along roads, trails, and riverbanks. The males regularly feed on moisture at such locations.

Host plants include *Brosimum alicastrum*, *Clarisia mexicana*, and *Maclura tinctoria*. Males and females feed on the nectar of *Lantana*, *Croton*, and *Cordia*. This species undergoes periodic increases in numbers that make them conspicuous to even the most casual observer. They sometimes migrate cross-country at the same time that the diurnal moth *Urania fulgens* is observed in migration.

WAITER DAGGERWING

The Waiter Daggerwing is commonly encountered at middle elevations in Costa Rica. It occurs in upper levels of lowland forests, in premontane, and in lower montane forests throughout the country. It lacks the longitudinal striping of most daggerwings. The back is a rather nondescript deep brown with paler brown edging on the outer portions of the wings. When at rest with the wings closed, the ventral surface of the wings discloses a bright white portion on the half of the wings closest to the body and a distinctly dark brown distal portion of the wings.

The host plants of this daggerwing are unknown, and the life history of the caterpillars is unrecorded. As with other daggerwings, the males visit mud puddles and wet sand to feed (often this is believed to occur where rainforest mammals have urinated on the sand). Both males and females feed on the nectar of rainforest plants like *Croton* and *Cordia*. The Waiter Daggerwing may sometimes be seen migrating across the country in the company of *Marpesia chiron* butterflies.

Marpesia coresia
Wingspread: 2.6–2.9 inches.
Range: Southern United States through South America.
Elevational range: 1,500–7,500 feet.

Waiter Daggerwing, wings closed

Waiter Daggerwing

MARPESIA MEROPS

Marpesia merops
Wingspread: 2.3–2.6 inches.
Range: Guatamala through South America.
Elevational range: Sea level to at least 5,100 feet.

Marpesia merops is a dark brown daggerwing with distinctive white spots on the forewings, well-developed tails, and several longitudinal dark brown stripes through the dorsal surface of the wings. Similar daggerwings in Costa Rica have either a light brown or an orange base color. This very widely distributed species can be found along riverbanks in moist and wet forests from sea level to over 9,000 feet. The host plants belong to the genus *Brosimum*. In southwestern Costa Rica, large *Brosimum* trees are referred to as milk trees because of their white sap. The butterflies are commonly observed on wet sand at the riverbanks, where they use their proboscis to imbibe moisture. This butterfly is known to participate in migratory movements.

Marpesia merops male

SUBFAMILY MORPHINAE

BLUE MORPHO

The stunning Blue Morpho is the most conspicuous and well-known rainforest butterfly.
Its swift, erratic flight and iridescent blue wings
create brilliant flashes of blue amid lush rainforest vegetation. This butterfly is frequently seen
along forest trails, on coffee and banana plantations, and along woodland streams in lowland and middle
elevations of the Caribbean and Pacific slopes. Most adults
in the Caribbean lowlands are iridescent blue on the dorsal
surface of the wings. In the southern Pacific lowlands they
have more brown on the wings, and some in the Central
Plateau are nearly all brown. In addition to *Morpho helenor*,
there are five other morphos in the country, including one
white species.

It is believed that the iridescent blue wings with
contrasting brown markings below serve as an effective
defense against predatory birds because the morpho's fast,
irregular dipsy-doodling flight makes the butterfly difficult to pursue. Because it has these escape strategies, the
morpho does not have toxins in its body like Heliconius
butterflies do. This butterfly is eaten by Rufous-tailed Jacamars and large flycatchers.

Morpho butterflies do not visit flowers. They feed only
on rotting fruits like bananas, on fruit peels, and on sap
that flows from cuts in the bark of trees and vines. Eggs
are laid singly on rainforest plants in the families Are-
caceae (genera *Astrocaryum* and *Geonoma*), Dichapeta-
laceae (genus *Dichapetalum*), Fabaceae (genera *Andira,
Dalbergia, Dioclea, Erythrina, Inga, Lonchocarpus, Macha-
erium, Platymiscium, Pterocarpus,* and *Sclerolobium*), Mal-
pighiaceae (genus *Heteropterys*), and Ochnaceae (genus
Ouratea). Newly hatched caterpillars are yellow and red.

Morphos can be observed in Tortuguero NP, La Selva
Biological Field Station, Braulio Carrillo NP, and at La
Virgen del Socorro on the Caribbean slope. On the Pacific
slope, they can be observed at Carara and Tapantí NPs,
Monteverde, Corcovado NP (including the Sirena Biologi-
cal Station), Corcovado Lodge Tent Camp, Tiskita Jungle
Lodge, and the Wilson Botanical Garden at San Vito.

Blue Morpho

*Morpho helenor marinita (formerly
Morpho peleides)*
Costa Rican names: *Celeste
común; morfo.*
Wingspread: 5.0–6.1 inches.
Range: Mexico to Colombia and
Venezuela.
Elevational range: Sea level to
5,100 feet.

Blue Morpho, wings closed

Blue Morpho caterpillar

Caligo brasiliensis sulanus adult, side view

Caligo brasiliensis sulanus
(formerly *Caligo sulanus*)
Costa Rican name: *Buhito pardo.*
Wingspread: 5.4–7.2 inches.
Range: Guatemala to Panama.
Elevational range: Sea level to 3,600 feet.

Caligo brasiliensis sulanus dorsal surface

Caligo brasiliensis sulanus ventral surface

CALIGO (OWL) BUTTERFLY

The huge Owl butterfly is one of the best-known insects of tropical lowland forests. The eyespot on the hindwing is the most conspicuous identification feature, and it is shared by all five species of *Caligo* in Costa Rica. Though primarily a rainforest butterfly, some species also occur in the dry forests of Guanacaste. The wingspread can exceed five inches, although this butterfly is typically observed with the wings closed as it rests on the side of a tree.

Caligo butterflies have an exceptional strategy for surviving attacks by birds. The eyespot provides a type of startle strategy for evading predatory birds. When a bird attacks, the eyespot startles the bird, disrupts the attack, and tricks the bird into attacking the eyespot rather than the real body of the butterfly. The butterfly has such huge wings that it can still fly to escape and live to reproduce even if the hindwing is damaged.

The caterpillars have two interesting survival adaptations. The young green caterpillars are inconspicuous because they align themselves along the main veins of leaves on host plants like *Heliconia,* banana (*Musa*), and *Calathea.* Before forming a pupa, they become conspicuous because of their size (over four inches long), but the larger caterpillars have a protective gland that is everted and used to release an offensive chemical when attacked. Owl butterflies are most active at dawn and dusk. They feed on rotting fruits like bananas, tree sap, mammal droppings, and even carrion. Adults may live up to five weeks.

Although banana plants are not native to Costa Rica, they are heavily used by *Caligo* caterpillars. This butterfly is considered an agricultural pest by banana growers. Caligo butterflies can be seen in Tortuguero NP and at La Selva Biological Field Station on the Caribbean slope. On the Pacific slope, look for them at Carara NP, Tiskita Jungle Lodge, Corcovado NP, and the Wilson Botanical Garden at San Vito.

Caligo brasiliensis sulanus eggs on banana leaf

Caligo brasiliensis sulanus, camouflaged caterpillar

Caligo brasiliensis sulanus, older caterpillars

CALIGO (OWL) BUTTERFLY

There are five species of Caligo (or Owl) butterflies in Costa Rica, and all are generally similar in their behavior and appearance, as described in the *Caligo brasiliensis* account. This Owl butterfly is better adapted to drier habitats and agricultural lands than is *C. brasiliensis sulanus,* which is associated more with rainforest environments. As such, it is more commonly associated with the dry forests of Guanacaste. Host plants include both *Heliconia* and *Musa* (bananas), but obviously bananas are not a common species in the dry forest region. In flight, it is apparent that the leading edges of the forewings are light brown and the posterior portions are black with some iridescent blue highlights near the body.

Caligo telamonius memnon
Costa Rican name: *Buhito pardo.*
Wingspread: 5.4–6.1 inches.
Range: Mexico to Brazil
Elevational range: Sea level to 3,600 feet.

Caligo telamonius memnon dorsal surface

CALIGO (OWL) BUTTERFLY

Caligo atreus dionysos
Wingspread: 2.9–6.7 inches.
Range: Costa Rica to Panama.
Elevational range: Sea level to
  4,800 feet.

Another Owl butterfly in the rainforest lowlands of Costa Rica, *Caligo atreus dionysos* is distinguished at rest by a bold pale diagonal bar across the wings. It can be identified in flight because the dorsal surface of the wings is purple with a band of creamy yellow along the outer edges of the hindwings.

Look for this butterfly in association with lowland rainforest environments and along forest, river, and wetland edges characterized by *Heliconia* plants, and also in the vicinity of banana plantations. It can be found in both the Caribbean lowlands and in the southern Pacific lowlands.

Caligo atreus dionysos, side view

Caligo atreus dionysos, with predator damage

PURPLE MORT BLEU

This large butterfly is found in the shady understory of lowland and premontane rainforest habitats, where at a distance, it gives the appearance of being a Caligo butterfly because of the bluish to purple markings on portions of the wings. At rest the wings quickly close to conceal the dorsal surfaces and a much more cryptic brownish ventral surface makes it hard to spot. There are small eyespots on the underside of the hindwing that are similar to but much smaller than those of the Caligo butterflies.

The host plants on which the caterpillars feed include members of the bamboo family (Poaceae), including *Lasiacis procerrima* and *Paspalum virgatum*. The Purple Mort Bleu is readily attracted to feed on rotten bananas at feeders in the tropical lowlands. The specimen shown here was attracted to overripe bananas at Tortuga Lodge in the Caribbean lowlands.

Eryphanis lycomedon (formerly
   Eryphanis polyxena lycomedon)
Wingspread: 3.6–4.1 inches.
Range: Guatemala to Brazil.
Elevational range: Sea level to
   2,400 feet.

Purple Mort Bleu, side view

SUBFAMILY SATYRINAE

PINK-TIPPED SATYR

Cithaerias pireta pireta
Wingspread: 2.3–2.5 inches.
Range: Mexico to Colombia.
Elevational range: Sea level to
6,000 feet.

Among butterflies, the Pink-tipped Satyr has one of the best strategies for avoiding predation. Its wings are transparent, so it blends into its surroundings whenever it lands. The hindwing has a rosy pink hue and a small eyespot that may tend to divert the attention of a potential predator from attacking the head and front parts of the butterfly.

The host plants of this beautiful little butterfly include *Philodendron rhodoaxis* and species of *Rhodospatha*. It is widespread at the ground level of rainforests where it inhabits light gaps in the forest and feeds on rotting fruits, like palm fruits, and rotting fungi. The specimen shown here was photographed on the grounds of the Bolívar Zoo in San José.

Pink-tipped Satyr

TYPHLA SATYR

The distinctively marked Typhla Satyr is easily identified because of the broad white longitudinal band that extends from the front edge of the forewing through the hindwing. Its distribution is limited to the premontane and lower levels of the lower montane moist and wet forests of the Caribbean slope. It is found in areas of high humidity and rainfall, including cloud forests.

The host plant, a type of cyperus called *Cyperus lazulae*, is characteristic of rainforests with swampy, wet habitats. The courtship of this butterfly is fascinating to watch. The male flies above the female, with the wings of both beating in synchrony. As the female descends to land, the male hovers above (as shown in the photo), and then he lands beside her. The male will touch the antennae of the female with his antennae as he vibrates his wings, and mating ensues.

The foods of this butterfly include rotting fruits and rotting fungi as well as animal droppings.

Typhla Satyr, side view

Oressinoma typhla
Wingspread: 1.6–1.9 inches.
Range: Costa Rica to Bolivia.
Elevational range: 2,100–3,600 feet.

Typhla Satyr male hovering over female

Monarch butterfly caterpillar

Danaus plexippus
Wingspread: 5.0–5.2 inches.
Range: Throughout the Americas; many other countries.
Elevational range: Sea level to 7,800 feet.

SUBFAMILY DANAINAE

MONARCH

The northern Monarch butterfly is probably the best-known butterfly in the Americas because of its migrations between North America and Mexico. Few people realize that there are also Monarchs to enjoy in Costa Rica. They are similar to their northern cousins, but they are not migratory. The only difference is a slight indentation in the sides of the forewings of northern migratory monarchs; on the Costa Rican variety the edge is fairly straight. The butterfly may be seen flitting along roadsides, pastures, and clearings from lowlands to lower montane elevations.

The tropical milkweed *Asclepias curassavica* is the primary host plant of the tropical Monarch, along with some other milkweeds and *Matelea* species. Adult Monarchs feed on the nectar of many flowers of forest openings, roadsides, and pastures, such as *Lantana*. The Monarch's bright orange color serves as a warning to predators of northern populations; the caterpillar has sequestered pyrrolizidine alkaloids in its system that make birds sick if the Monarch is eaten.

In North America this has given rise to a classic example of Batesian mimicry. The Viceroy butterfly has no distasteful qualities, but birds avoid it because it looks similar to the inedible Monarch. There are no comparable Batesian mimicry complexes involving Monarchs in the tropics, and it is not known if the tropical Monarchs are as distasteful as northern Monarchs. There are, however, several species of butterflies in the same genus as the Monarch, and they all have host plants that could provide them with the same powerful chemicals that Monarchs appear to possess. This would suggest that the tropical Monarch is part of a multispecies Müllerian mimicry complex. The specimen shown here was photographed in the pastures of Rancho Naturalista near Tuis.

Monarch butterfly

SUBFAMILY ITHOMIINAE

GLASSWING BUTTERFLY

Greta morgane is one of the most common of more than twenty small clearwing butterflies in the subfamily Ithomiinae. The transparent wings make it difficult for a predatory bird to track it in flight. An insect of middle elevations, this butterfly is regularly encountered in gardens around San José and forest openings and disturbed habitats of the Caribbean and Pacific slopes. This clearwing undergoes elevational migratory movements and at times can be very abundant.

Adults visit common flowers like *Lantana*. Eggs are laid on plants of the nightshade family (Solanaceae), including species in the genera *Cestrum* and *Solanum*. From these plants the caterpillars acquire toxic alkaloids and an undesirable taste that discourages predation by birds. The pupae of this butterfly are silver, which contributes to its Costa Rican name *espejitos,* meaning "little mirrors." The caterpillars develop into very toxic adults; their taste and the effects on birds that eat them also discourage predation.

Greta morgane oto (formerly Greta oto)
Costa Rican name: *Espejitos.*
Wingspread: 2.2–2.4 inches.
Range: Mexico to Panama.
Elevational range: Sea level to 3,900 feet.

Glasswing butterfly, side view

Glasswing butterfly chrysalis

HERALDICA CLEARWING

Ithomia heraldica heraldica
Wingspread: 2.2–2.4 inches.
Range: Nicaragua to Panama.
Elevational range: 300–5,400 feet.

This Clearwing butterfly is known mainly from middle elevations on the Pacific slope above 3,000 feet. It is uncommon on the Caribbean slope and in the lowlands. The markings of this butterfly appear similar to Heliconius butterflies, but the wings have a semi-transparent quality.

Host plants are in the nightshade family (Solanaceae), including *Solanum lanceifolium, Solanum pertenue,* and *Witheringia riparia.* These butterflies appear to acquire pyrrolizidine alkaloids from host plants, causing them to taste bad to avian predators. This may explain why some species in this genus resemble *Heliconius* and *Eueides* butterflies; they are apparently part of an intergeneric Müllerian mimicry complex, in which the butterflies resemble each other and all taste bad to birds.

Another host plant of this butterfly, *Acnistus arborescens,* is commonly planted as a shade tree on shade coffee plantations. The butterfly can therefore be abundant in coffee plantations. The Heraldica Clearwing feeds on the nectar of common flowers like *Stachytarpheta, Impatiens,* and *Lantana.* They will also feed on juices from bird droppings.

Heraldica Clearwing

ORANGE-SPOTTED TIGER CLEARWING

The Orange-spotted Tiger Clearwing is one of the most common butterflies in Costa Rica. It may be encountered in dry, moist, and wet forests as well as deforested lands, pastures, plantations, and city gardens. One interesting feature of this butterfly is that its seasonal migrations are elevational, traveling up and down mountainous areas.

Another orange, black, and yellow butterfly that resembles many *Heliconius* and *Eueides* species, this clearwing appears to be an example of a bad-tasting butterfly in this large Müllerian mimicry complex. Host plants include members of the nightshade family (Solanaceae), including *Solanum* and *Physalis* species. Males visit flowers that contain pyrrolizidine alkaloids that may contribute to their bad taste, but this is mainly conjecture, because the biochemistry and natural history of this genus and species remain to be studied in detail.

Orange-spotted Tiger Clearwing, side view

Mechanitis polymnia isthmia
Wingspread: 2.5–2.8 inches.
Range: Mexico to Brazil.
Elevational range: Sea level to 3,600 feet.

Orange-spotted Tiger Clearwing female

PTERONYMIA FULVIMARGO

Pteronymia fulvimargo (formerly
Pteronymia notilla)
Wingspread: 1.8–2.1 inches.
Range: Costa Rica to Colombia.
Elevational range: 2,100–6,000 feet.

This small forest butterfly of middle elevations can be seen in sunny sites along forest edges and roadsides. Host plants are members of the nightshade family (Solanaceae), including *Solanum rovirosanum, S. brenesii,* and *S. arboreum.* The insects are believed to sequester pyrrolizidine alkaloids in their system, making them taste bad to birds that would otherwise eat them. The orange, black, and yellow markings of the female suggest that it is part of the large Müllerian mimicry complex that includes many *Heliconius, Eueides, Mechanitis, Greta,* and *Ithomia* butterflies.

Pteronymia fulvimargo, side view

MOTHS

Moths are not as conspicuous as monkeys or macaws in the forests of Costa Rica, but they represent a major component of the nation's biodiversity. Taxonomists at the National Biodiversity Institute (INBIO) have estimated that Costa Rica has 1,400 to 2,100 butterflies and an incredible 11,900 to 12,600 species of moths. This includes a variety of beautiful and fascinating insects that range in size from over seven inches in wingspread to microscopic moths smaller than a fingernail.

The word "moth" applies generally to members of the order Lepidoptera that usually have complex, featherlike antennae. Butterflies, in contrast, have simpler clublike antennae. Of course, like most things in nature, there are exceptions. Moths of the family Castniidae look like butterflies and have clublike antennae. Costa Rica has seventy-three families in the order Lepidoptera, and among those, only five are typically considered butterflies.

Most moths are nocturnal and so are missed by Costa Rican tourists who spend long active days in pursuit of monkeys, birds, flowers, and butterflies, only to collapse into bed when the night shift of moths comes out. Moths represent a wonderful but largely unknown and unappreciated group of insects. For instance, some sphinx moths have extremely long tongues that are a special adaptation for

Moth collection specimens

Daniel Acuerdas, INBIO parataxonomist

Tongue of Sphinx moth

Nicotiana blossom, example of a moth-pollinated flower

pollinating flowers with extremely long corollas. Without those moths, those flowers would not survive in nature.

In the future, more effort will be required to unravel secrets of the life histories of moths, including determination of their host plants. Dr. Daniel H. Janzen and Winnie Hallwachs of the University of Pennsylvania have spent a lifetime studying, collecting, and researching the life histories of moths in the Guanacaste Conservation Area. Much of what we know about their ecology, host plants, parasites, and relationships to other species is the result of their pioneering work. If you wish to learn more about Costa Rican moths, go to their Web site at http://janzen.sas.upenn.edu.

The author encourages Costa Rican travelers to look for moths and other nocturnal insects at the security lights of their lodges. They should encourage lodges to provide black lights and sheets on their grounds to attract moths so that the beauty and diversity of moths can be enjoyed while visiting the American tropics.

MEGALOPYGE MOTH

Megalopyge is an intriguing and primitive genus of moths found from the southern United States to Central America. Its species have long, soft-looking fur that resembles a fluffy Persian cat, resulting in the nickname "pussy moth." The caterpillar may be golden to grayish in color, and there may be an orange streak down the back. Beneath the furry hair of this caterpillar are urticating spines that can deliver painful stings and severe medical problems (including unconsciousness) to anyone who touches them. Host plants include at least seventeen genera and twenty-seven species, among them *Inga, Quercus* (oaks), *Mimosa, Miconia, Piper,* and *Cordia* trees. Instead of creating a chrysalis, this caterpillar pupates inside the furry coat of its last larval stage and emerges as an adult. The grayish, orangish, yellowish adult moth looks so fluffy that it is hard to believe that it could fly.

Megalopyge spp.
Wingspread: 0.9–1.4 inches.
Range: Southern United States to Central America.
Elevational range: Sea level to about 6,000 feet.

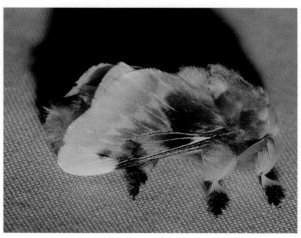

Megalopyge moth

CASTNIOMERA ATYMNIUS FUTILIS

Castniomera atymnius futilis
Wingspread: 2.0–2.1 inches.
Range: Mexico to Brazil.
Elevational range: Sea level to
   3,900 feet.

This diurnal moth can be confusing to the amateur observer because it looks like a butterfly but is not in the butterfly identification guides. A day-flying moth, it is medium to dark brown with pale whitish lines through the forewings. When at rest, the white markings of the hindwings are partially concealed and reveal a heart-shaped marking that looks like a white valentine.

The distribution of this moth includes the Caribbean lowlands up to premontane forests of the Cordillera of Guanacaste and Cordillera of Tilarán.

This species has been observed twice along the loop nature trail behind Tortuga Lodge in the Caribbean lowlands. Little information is available for this species.

Castniomera atymnius

SUBFAMILY OXYTENINAE

DEAD-LEAF MOTH

A fascinating member of the saturnid family, the Dead-leaf moth has two great strategies for survival. The large caterpillar has a smooth green body. If threatened, it can inflate its body to look like a snake's head, with huge eyespots, deterring potential predators from eating it.

The adult moth has a cryptic bicolored pattern of tan to pale brown or grayish over the wings, with a horizontal line that breaks up the pattern of the moth. The horizontal line simulates the midvein of a dead leaf. This moth was photographed on the grounds of Tortuga Lodge in the Caribbean lowlands.

Oxytenis modestia caterpillar, showing false eyespots. Photo by Dan Janzen.

Oxytenis modestia
Wingspread: 2.1–2.3 inches.
Range: Guatemala to Brazil.
Elevational range: Sea level to 4,900 feet.

Oxytenis modestia male

SUBFAMILY ARSENURINAE

Rhescyntis hippodamia
Wingspread: 7.5 inches.
Range: Mexico to Brazil.
Elevational range: Sea level to
about 5,000 feet.

RHESCYNTIS HIPPODAMIA

This is one of the largest moths in Costa Rica, with a wingspread of more than seven inches. The wings have a handsome pattern of brown markings shading to pinkish. The moth comes to night lights, and it has been encountered at middle elevations, at sites like Rancho Naturalista on the Caribbean slope and the Wilson Botanical Garden on the Pacific slope near the Panama border. The host plant for this beautiful moth is *Virola koschynyi,* in the family Myristicaceae. This moth is found at lower and middle elevations in rainforest wherever *Virola* trees are found.

Rhescyntis hippodamia male

SUBFAMILY CERATOCAMPINAE

IMPERIAL MOTH

The beautiful Imperial moth is one of the most stunning saturnid moths. The soft colors of yellow and purple and the large size of the moth are sure to impress even the most casual nature tourist. The North American distribution of this species ranges from Canada to Latin America.

This moth is broadly distributed in Costa Rica at lower and middle elevations and in habitats ranging from dry forests to rainforests. It is also found at higher elevations where the caterpillars feed on oaks (*Quercus*) in the montane forests of the Talamanca Mountains. Dr. Daniel H. Janzen has discovered recently, however, that moths of the Guanacaste dry forest that have long been thought to be *Eacles imperialis* actually belong to a different, newly identified species. They look similar, but *Eacles imperialis decoris* occupies the wetter rainforest environments.

One factor that explains the broad distribution of this moth is its use of a large number of host plants in a wide variety of plant families. In Costa Rica this species has been documented to use host plants in the families Cochlospermaceae (*Cochlospermum*), Elaeocarpaceae (*Sloanea*), Fabaceae (*Erythrina* and *Lonchocarpus*), Melastomaceae (*Conostegia*), Myrtaceae (*Psidium*), Sapindaceae (*Thouinidium*), and Lamiaceae (*Gmelina arborea*). The look-alike species uses a different combination of host plants. Further information on *Eacles imperialis* and its host plants in Costa Rica is available on Dr. Janzen's Web site at http://janzen.sas.upenn.edu.

Eacles imperialis decoris
Wingspread: 3.1–6.8 inches.
Range: Mexico to Costa Rica.
Elevational range: Sea level to about 4,000 feet.

Imperial moth male

ORMONDEI IMPERIAL MOTH

Eacles ormondei
Wingspread: 4.1 inches.
Range: Mexico to Bolivia.
Elevational range: Sea level to about 5,100 feet.

The distribution of *Eacles ormondei* includes moist and wet forests of tropical upper premontane and lower montane levels of the Caribbean slope of Costa Rica, middle elevations of the Pacific slope near the Panama border, and the Osa Peninsula.

This rainforest species of Imperial moth utilizes a variety of host plants in seven families: Anacardiaceae, Malvaceae, Meliaceae, Myrsinaceae, Proteaceae, Rosaceae, and Sabiaceae.

Ormondei Imperial moth male

SUBFAMILY HEMICEUCINAE

AUTOMERIS BANUS

Automeris banus male

Within the saturnid family of moths is a prominent genus represented by 264 species, and that number continues to grow as new species are identified within and among existing species. These are the moths often referred to in northern regions as Io moths. They are medium-sized, with yellowish colors and prominent eyespots on the hindwings. The eyespots discourage avian predators from attacking them. These species show a cryptic dead-leaf pattern when their wings are closed. If alarmed by a predator, the wings open to disclose a dramatic pair of eyespots that can startle a potential predator into thinking that a larger creature like an owl might be ready to attack them. This can allow the moth enough time to escape. One reason that this genus is so widespread in the Americas, from Canada to South America, is that the species are able to utilize many genera as host plants.

Automeris banus banus
Wingspread: About 3.1 inches.
Range: Mexico to Ecuador.
Elevational range: Sea level to 5,400 feet.

Among the significant qualities of the *Automeris* moths is that their caterpillars have urticating spines, which can cause painful and irritating wounds. Many caterpillars in Costa Rica have urticating hairs or spines to deter attacking predators. They can also be quite painful to curious tourists.

Throughout the more northerly range of *A. banus*, host plants include sumacs, willows, plums, beech, oaks, and privet. Oaks, a temperate species found at higher elevations in Costa Rica, would serve as host plants for this attractive moth.

Automeris zugana male, wings open, showing eyespots

Automeris zugana
Wingspread: About 3.1 inches.
Range: Costa Rica to Peru.
Elevational range: Sea level to 5,400 feet.

Automeris zugana, wings closed, showing camouflage pattern

AUTOMERIS ZUGANA

Automeris zugana is another saturnid moth with distinctive eyeball markings on the hindwings. The overall color of the forewings is pale tan, in contrast to the medium brown of *A. banus* and the dark gray of *A. postalbida.* The base color of the hindwings surrounding the eyespots is pale yellow on *A. zugana,* rich pinkish orange on *A. banus,* and pale cream on *A. postalbida.* The proximal area of the hindwings near the body is pinkish-orange.

The moth traditionally recognized as *A. zugana* has recently been discovered to be at least three different but similar species. Genetic barcoding studies by Dr. Daniel H. Janzen in Guanacaste National Park have revealed that the moths originally recognized as *A. zugana* utilize 29 species from fifteen plant families. Among the primary host plants are species of *Inga* in the family Fabaceae. A second similar species utilizes 138 host plant species in 42 plant families. A third look-alike species uses 16 host plant species in nine plant families, and a fourth uses 26 host plant species in eighteen plant families.

The main point of this account is to highlight that Costa Rica's butterflies and moths are the result of millions of years of natural selection and adaptation to unique combinations of host plants that allow for their survival. The outward appearance of many apparent species is sometimes inadequate to reveal the genetic secrets of these adaptations, which have resulted in complexes of similar-looking species. Thanks to the pioneering research of scientists like Dr. Daniel Janzen and parataxonomists at INBIO, the genetic codes and species composition of Costa Rica's tropical habitats are being decoded.

AUTOMERIS POSTALBIDA

Another of Costa Rica's attractive Io moths, *Automeris postalbida* has a dark gray, charcoal base color on the forewings. The eyespots on the hindwings are surrounded by a cream-colored background. The eyespot has a black ring at its periphery and a narrow white bar in the center. This species is found from Costa Rica to Peru. As with *A. zugana,* it belongs to a complex of species that each utilizes a different combination of host plants. One species uses ninety-eight plant species in thirty-seven genera (including species in the families Euphorbiaceae, Fabaceae, Rubiaceae, and Urticaceae); a look-alike uses ninety-two host plant species in thirty-seven genera (including the families Euphorbiaceae, Meliaceae, Sabiaceae, and Urticaceae). Additional species are also believed to exist and may be revealed by further host plant studies and genetic barcoding research.

Automeris postalbida
Wingspread: About 3.1 inches.
Range: Costa Rica to Ecuador.
Elevational range: Sea level to 4,800 feet.

Automeris postalbida female

PSEUDODIRPHIA MENANDER

Pseudodirphia menander
Wingspread: 2.8 inches.
Range: Nicaragua to Ecuador.
Elevational range: 1,800–3,700 feet.

One of the most colorful saturnid moths in Costa Rica is a medium-sized moth known as *Pseudodirphia menander*. It has pink forewings and gray hindwings with a white stripe through both sets of wings. The thorax and abdomen are deep orange with black bands on the abdomen. The host plant is a common rainforest vine in the family Araceae, *Monstera tenuis*. The moth is attracted to night lights and is found in middle elevation moist and wet forests.

Pseudodirphia menander male

SUBFAMILY SATURNIINAE

LEBEAU'S ROTHSCHILDIA SILKMOTH

Rothschildia silkmoths are among the largest of Costa Rican moths. The transparent patches in the forewings and hindwings, like triangular windows, distinguish them from other moths. *R. lebeau* has grayish wings with white, black, and brown highlights. The female's wings are more rounded than those of the male. The host plants of *R. lebeau* include *Zanthoxylum, Salix,* and *Prunus.* The adults do not feed. Adults of *R. lebeau* emerge from their cocoons in early evening and mate from about 10:00 PM to midnight. Egg laying begins on the following night and continues for several more nights. In the Guanacaste dry forest, *R. lebeau* can produce two generations of offspring during the rainy season from May through December. In the rainforest, adult *Rothschildia* silkmoths can be found throughout the year. They have been encountered at night lights at Monteverde Lodge and Rancho Naturalista.

Rothschildia lebeau
Wingspread: 4.5–5.3 inches.
Range: Rio Grande Valley of Texas to Brazil.
Elevational range: Sea level to 3,200 feet.

Rothschildia lebeau

ROTHSCHILDIA TRILOBA SILKMOTH

Rothschildia triloba
Wingspread: 4.5–5.3 inches.
Range: Rio Grande Valley of Texas to Brazil.
Elevational range: Sea level to 4,500 feet.

A rainforest species of middle and upper elevations, the Triloba silkmoth is larger and more reddish than *Rothschildia lebeau*. It is not a species of tropical dry forests. This species can be confused with *R. orizaba,* which is found only at very high elevations. The adult moth does not feed.

Host plants of this species include members of many plant families: Anacardiaceae, Aquifoliaceae, Araliaceae, Burseraceae, Caprifoliaceae, Euphorbiaceae, Moraceae, Rosaceae, Rubiaceae, Rutaceae, Salicaceae, and Simaroubaceae. This suggests that it is broadly adapted to survive in many different habitats.

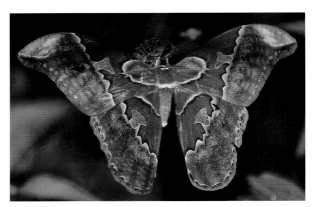

Rothschildia triloba

ANTHERAEA GODMANI

The large and impressive Saturniid moth known as *Antheraea godmani* is found in Costa Rica's highlands, where the large, spiny caterpillars are able to feed on oak leaves in the montane forests. Like other members of this family, the adults do not feed. After hatching from a cocoon, the female attracts males with a powerful phero-mone and mates once. The female then lays its fertilized eggs and dies within six to eight days. This specimen was photographed at Savegre Mountain Lodge in the San Gerardo de Dota Valley of Cerro de la Muerte. The other large silkmoth encountered at this high elevation is *Roth-schildia triloba*.

Antheraea godmani
Wingspread: 5.9 inches.
Range: Mexico to Guatemala.
Elevational range: 3,000–6,900 feet.

Antheraea godmani male

COPAXA RUFINANS

Copaxa rufinans
Wingspread: 3.0–3.5 inches.
Range: Mexico to Ecuador.
Elevational range: Sea level to 5,100 feet.

Among Costa Rica's beautiful and cryptically marked saturnid moths are members of the genus *Copaxa*. These moths have patterns of brown with a tiny transparent window in each wing.

The host plants for *Copaxa rufinans* are members of the avocado family (Lauraceae), including *Persea*, *Nectandra salicina*, *Ocotea*, *Licaria*, and *Beilschmiedia*. The distribution of this species extends primarily in rainforest habitats at middle elevations from the Nicaragua border to Panama.

Copaxa rufinans female

Copaxa rufinans male

COPAXA SYNTHERATOIDES

This large Saturniid moth is found in moist and wet for- est habitats at middle and higher elevations in Costa Rica. It depends on host plants of both native and cultivated species of avocados in the family Lauraceae (*Nectandra* and *Persea*). This specimen was photographed at Savegre Mountain Lodge at an elevation of about 7,200 feet.

Copaxa syntheratoides
Wingspread: 3.0–3.5 inches.
Range: Mexico to Ecuador.
Elevational range: 2,400–9,600 feet.

Copaxa syntheratoides male

THERINIA TRANSVERSARIA

*Therinia transversaria (formerly
Asthenidia transversaria)*
Wingspread: 2.8 inches.
Range: Nicaragua to Colombia.
Elevation: Sea level to 4,500 feet.

One of the most beautiful silkmoths in Costa Rica is this small species with an immaculate white appearance, soft gray bars through the wings, and orange and black spots on the posterior tips of the hindwings. It is not as large as the *Rothschildia* silkmoths, and it does not have the transparent windows in its wings, so it may not be immediately recognized as a silkmoth. This attractive species is found from Nicaragua to Colombia.

Like other silkmoths, it does not feed as an adult. The caterpillars feed on host plants in the coffee family (Rubiaceae). The caterpillar has imposing eyespots similar to those of the Dead-leaf moth, *Oxytenis modestia*. The species is attracted to lights at night. Among locations where it may be encountered are La Selva, La Virgen del Socorro, the vicinity of Volcano Arenal, and Rancho Naturalista in the Caribbean lowlands. In the Pacific lowlands it has been recorded at the Wilson Botanical Garden at San Vito and at Sirena in Corcovado NP.

Therinia transversaria

SUBFAMILY MACROGLOSSINAE

XYLOPHANES TITANA

This Sphinx moth with the swept-wing look readily comes to night lights. Its host plants include members of the coffee family (Rubiaceae), like *Manettia reclinata*.

The large green caterpillar of this species has two false eyespots that would tend to discourage potential predators. See Dr. Daniel Janzen's Web site for photos of the imposing caterpillar (http://janzen.sas.upenn.edu). Click on "Caterpillars, Pupae, Butterflies, and Moths of the ACG."

The moth specimen shown here was photographed at Rancho Naturalista near Tuis.

Xylophanes titana
Wingspread: 3.5–3.7 inches.
Range: Mexico to Costa Rica.
Elevational range: Sea level to 6,000 feet.

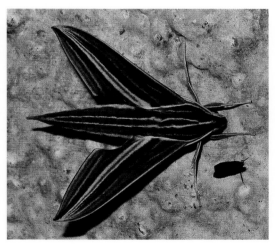

Xylophanes titana

MADORYX PLUTONIUS

Madoryx plutonius plutonius
Wingspread: 3.6–4.7 inches.
Range: Costa Rica to Brazil.
Elevational range: Sea level to 6,300 feet.

A heavy-bodied Sphinx moth commonly encountered at night lights in Costa Rica, *Madoryx plutonius* has a small, distinctive white crescent in the center of each brown forewing. The host plant of this moth is *Conostegia xalapensis*. The caterpillar has a fascinating defense against predation. Its colors provide camouflage, but it has a large false head, with eyes and a face, that looks like the head of a snake. This helps deter potential predators. A photo of the caterpillar can be seen at http://janzen.sas.upenn. edu. Click on "Caterpillars, Pupae, Butterflies, and Moths of the ACG."

Madoryx plutonius male

BANDED SPHINX MOTH

The Banded Sphinx is a common and distinctive rainforest moth that comes to night lights in Costa Rica. Marks that look like racing stripes on the forewings and pinkish highlights on the hindwings help distinguish it from a look-alike moth, *Eumorpha vitis*. The host plants for the caterpillars include *Fuchsia* and *Ludwigia*. The caterpillars are quite stunning. Like most other moth caterpillars, they go through five stages of development, called instars. They can be pink or greenish with diagonal whitish bars on the sides, and the fifth instar has a dramatic pattern of black, red, green, and whitish markings, still highlighted by about eight whitish diagonal markings on the sides, or they may remain green. Go to http://janzen.sas.upenn.edu to see the great variety of caterpillar markings. Click on "Caterpillars, Pupae, Butterflies, and Moths of the ACG."

Eumorpha fasciatus fasciatus
Wingspread: 3.4–3.8 inches.
Range: Mexico to Argentina.
Elevational range: Sea level to 5,100 feet.

Banded Sphinx male

SUBFAMILY SMERINTHINAE

Adhemarius ypsilon
Wingspread: 3.6–4.9 inches.
Range: Mexico to Argentina.
Elevational range: Sea level to 4,800 feet.

ADHEMARIUS YPSILON

The Sphinx moth *Adhemarius ypsilon* is grayish, with a bold black bar across the back extending to the leading edge of each forewing, and the hindwings are rosy pink, with black markings featuring pink ovals inside black edging. This moth commonly comes to night lights in Costa Rica. Its host plants include members of the wild avocado family (Lauraceae), including *Ocotea atirrensis, O. dendrodaphne, O. nicaraguensis, O. veraguensis, Persea,* and *Nectandra.* The caterpillars show considerable variation and may have striking lime-green, blue and green, or yellow patterns. See Dr. Janzen's Web site for photos, http:// janzen.sas.upenn.edu. Click on "Caterpillars, Pupae, Butterflies, and Moths of the ACG."

Adhemarius ypsilon

SUBFAMILY URANIINAE

GREEN PAGE MOTH (GREEN URANIA)

The green jewellike iridescence and elegant swallowtail design of the diurnal Green Page moth make it one of the most stunning lepidopterans in Costa Rica. Most people consider it a butterfly because it flies during the day, but it is a diurnal moth. This moth has its origins primarily in the wet swamps and forests of the Osa Peninsula, where its host plant is abundant. The plant is a rainforest vine in the euphorbia (spurge) family called *Omphalea diandra*.

Green Page moth

Urania fulgens
Costa Rican name: *Colipato verde*.
Wingspread: 2.3–3.2 inches.
Range: Veracruz, Mexico, to Brazil.
Elevational Range: Sea level to at least 6,000 feet.

The breeding season begins in May, and up to five generations may be produced before the end of the rainy season in November to December. Every few years there is an enormous migration of this moth across the country. Hundreds of thousands fly from the Osa Peninsula across the Central Plateau into the lowlands north of San Carlos, and others fly from breeding areas in Panama through Costa Rica's Caribbean lowlands and along the coast. Others fly from Guatemala south to Colombia. The migration begins in July to August and may last several months. The frequency of migrations may be every four to eight years. Very large migrations occurred in 1969, 1983, 1995, 1998, and 2005. As the moths stage for migration in the forests of Corcovado NP, thousands can blanket the trees in much the same way that Monarchs cover roosting trees during migration in North America.

The reason for the migration seems related to the extent to which the *Urania* caterpillars eat the *Omphalea* leaves. These leaves provide a low amount of toxic chemicals that the caterpillar incorporates into its system to discourage predation. As the amount of foraging increases, however, the plants begin producing higher concentrations of toxic chemicals that can subsequently kill the caterpillars. Adults must then move to a new region where the vines have not recently been exploited by this moth. In March following a migration, there is a much smaller migration back to the original breeding area. Adults feed primarily on the nectar of white flowers like *Inga*, *Leucania*, *Eupatorium*, and guava (*Psidium*). The female may lay clusters of up to eighty eggs on *Omphalea* leaves.

SUBFAMILY CATOCALINAE

BLACK WITCH

Ascalapha odorata (formerly Erebus odora)
Costa Rican name: *Bruja negra.*
Wingspread: 5.9 inches.
Range: South Florida to Brazil.
Elevational range: Sea level to 9,900 feet.

The Black Witch is a great traveler and is so adaptable that it is found from Florida to Brazil. It can be encountered at night lights in coastal areas at sea level and high in the Andes of South America. This large brown moth has a dark comma-shaped mark on each forewing, and females have a prominent purplish-pink bar across each forewing and hindwing. The name "Black Witch" apparently comes from Mexican folklore, which suspiciously considers it the "butterfly of death."

Adults feed at night on overripe fruit like bananas and on native fruits high in the rainforest canopy. It can be attracted to lights at night. By day it roosts in dark sheltered places like hollow trees and rocky crevices. It is most abundant during the rainy season but also survives well during the dry season in moist microhabitats of forests along rivers and shaded ravines.

Host plants are primarily in the bean family (Fabaceae): *Mora*, *Cassia*, *Acacia*, and *Pithecellobium*. This moth undergoes sporadic dispersal movements each year from August to October into the United States. It can show up in states ranging from California to Minnesota and New York. There is even a record from Canada.

Black Witch female

A fascinating group of moths, the family Arctiidae includes nearly 600 species in Costa Rica. Many species are masters of disguise and heavily loaded with weapons of chemical warfare for defense against predators. Although these are moths, many are diurnal because they are Müllerian mimics of distasteful diurnal butterflies. Other members of this family mimic wasps in order to discourage predation by birds. Some of these moths have conspicuous yellow, orange, and black markings that resemble Heliconius butterflies, and others are brightly colored with iridescent red or iridescent blue as a warning to birds.

This is one very toxic family of moths. The chemicals responsible for their nasty taste are sequestered in their bodies during the caterpillar stage, when they feed on the foliage of plants in families like Apocynaceae and Euphorbiaceae. Chemicals from those plants are synthesized into pyrrolizidines, cardenolides, and histamines that smell and taste bad to any birds that try to eat them. These chemicals will not kill the birds, but birds tend to remember that eating such brightly colored lepidopterans will make them very sick.

The life histories of many species in this family are poorly known, but they are generally recognizable as members of the family Arctiidae. Among three tribes in the subfamily Arctiinae are Arctiini, Pericopini, and Ctenuchini. Three examples in those tribes have been selected for general coverage here, but they are included without detailed species accounts.

SUBFAMILY ARCTIINAE

TRIBE ARCTIINI (LEOPARD MOTHS)

Moths of this tribe are typically marked with patterns of black, yellow, and orange; they are Müllerian mimics of the Heliconius butterflies, which also taste bad to birds. They will come to lights at night. The individual shown here was photographed at a night light at Rancho Naturalista.

Chetone angulosa, a leopard moth in the tribe Arctiini

TRIBE CTENUCHINI (CTENUCHID MOTHS)

Ctenuchid moths are masters of disguise. Highly modi-
fied diurnal moths, they masquerade as wasps. Some
have transparent wasplike windows on their wings and
iridescent scales on the wings and body that mimic the
iridescence of wasps. Because birds avoid being stung by
wasps, the moths' resemblance to wasps discourages birds
from attacking them. The ctenuchid moth shown here, a
Macroneme species, was photographed at a night light at
Rancho Naturalista.

Ctenuchid moths, including this species in the genus *Macroneme*, mimic wasps

TRIBE PERICOPINI (PERICOPID MOTHS)

Pericopid moths are highly specialized. Frequently brightly colored with warning patterns, some are Müllerian mimics of bad-tasting butterflies. Like many other moths in this family, the caterpillars feed on plants in the family Apocynaceae, among others. From these plants they create toxic and bad-tasting chemicals that make the adults undesirable prey for birds. *Hypocrita aletta* has conspicuous iridescent pale blue markings along the margins of the wings, which would also serve as a warning to birds of its toxic qualities.

Hypocrita aletta, a brightly colored moth in the tribe Pericopini

OTHER INVERTEBRATES

Invertebrates other than butterflies and moths constitute the bulk of Costa Rica's biological diversity. There are tens of thousands of invertebrates in every life zone and at every level of the forest that are even now poorly known and largely unidentified. Ants, bees, beetles, bugs, wasps, katydids, and thousands of microscopic invertebrates are a rich heritage of Costa Rica's tropical forests. One study in Panama revealed that 950 species of beetles inhabited a single rainforest tree, so single trees are habitat for thousands of insects. The National Biodiversity Institute (INBIO) is making huge efforts to collect, catalog, and identify the country's invertebrates. Of the estimated 505,000 species in the country, 1,481 are vertebrates, 10,000 are plants, and the remaining 493,000-plus species are invertebrates. The twenty-four creatures featured here are only a tiny sampler of Costa Rica's invertebrate fauna and are included because they traditionally capture the attention of wildlife travelers.

Harlequin beetle close-up

Lichen katydid (Markia hystrix) lives among greenish lichens.

Leaf-mimic katydid (*Mimetica sp.*) appears as a dead leaf.

GIANT DAMSELFLY FAMILY *(Pseudostigmatidae)*

HELICOPTER DAMSELFLY (GIANT DAMSELFLY)

*Mecistogaster spp. and
Megaloprepus caerulatus*
Costa Rican name: *Gallito azul.*
Wingspread: 7.5 inches.
Length: 4 inches.
Range: Mexico to Brazil.
Elevational range: Sea level to at
least 3,900 feet.

Mecistogaster spp.

Megaloprepus caerulatus

Helicopter damselflies are one of the most mystifying—
and enchanting—insects of the rainforest. These huge
damselflies defy all logical explanations for the principles
of flight, because the four wings appear to beat slowly in
four directions at once and at different rates as the damselfly floats through the air among forest understory plants.

There are two genera of helicopter damselflies. The
genus *Mecistogaster* is characterized by clear wings that
have yellow tips. It includes three species in Costa Rica:
M. linearis, M. modesta, and *M. ornata. M. linearis* is
found from sea level to about 600 feet, only in the Caribbean lowlands. *M. modesta* is found from sea level to
3,600 feet, in moist and wet forests of both the Caribbean
slope and the southern Pacific slope. The third species,
M. ornata, is found from sea level to 3,300 feet along the
entire Pacific slope but not on the Caribbean slope.

Megaloprepus caerulatus is found at middle elevations
of the Caribbean slope, from about 600 to 3,300 feet, and
has been observed at La Selva. It has blue to purple bands
on its clear wings. The male has a white patch in front of
the bluish patch. Examples of good places to see helicopter
damselflies are the Arboretum at La Selva Biological Field
Station, the rainforests of Tortuguero NP, and Corcovado

Megaloprepus caerulatus male

NP on the Osa Peninsula. This species is the largest dam-selfly in the world, with a wingspread of 6.4 inches. It may also be observed at Carara NP and at higher elevations in the premontane forests of the Wilson Botanical Garden near San Vito.

The eggs of this genus are laid in the water tanks of bromeliads and in water-filled tree holes. The predatory nymphs mature in these tiny water reservoirs, where they eat small aquatic organisms like mosquito larvae. Larger larvae eat tadpoles of frogs and syrphid fly larvae. They also eat larvae of their own species, which reduces com-petition for limited food resources in these small water cavities. Since there are about 250 tropical species of wild-life that complete at least part of their life cycle in these bromeliad water tanks, there is apparently no shortage of food for predatory damselfly larvae. The larvae develop over a period of four to eight months.

Mecistogaster sp.

Adult damselflies prey on spiders. The transparent wings make them largely invisible to spiders resting on their webs. The damselfly hovers a couple of feet from the spider as it prepares to attack. With great swiftness and agility, the damselfly swoops at the spider and captures it with its forelegs. It then flies backward from the web and goes to a nearby perch, where it consumes the entire spi-der except the legs.

Megaloprepus caerulatus female

SUBFAMILY ROMALEINAE

Tropidacris cristata
Costa Rican names: *Saltamonte;*
  chapulín gigante.
Length: 2.5–3.0 inches.
Range: Mexico to Brazil.
Elevational range: Sea level to
  5,100 feet.

GIANT RED-WINGED GRASSHOPPER

The Giant Red-winged grasshopper is one of the largest grasshoppers in the world. The species can approach three inches in length, with a wingspread of nearly seven inches. Larger specimens have been reported over five inches long. Since the wings are deep red, these grasshoppers are very conspicuous when they flush. This rainforest species can be found throughout much of Costa Rica, but it is rarely encountered.

H. F. Rowell (1983) has reported that this grasshopper has been found in association with plants of the genus *Quassia.* The author has encountered the wings of this grasshopper at night security lights at the Wilson Botanical Garden, where birds apparently caught and ate the grasshoppers when they came to the lights at night. The grasshoppers have also been observed in the gardens of Hotel Cristal Ballena on the southern Pacific coast. You will know this grasshopper when you see it; it is almost big enough to trip over.

Grasshopper wings left by a bird predator

Giant Red-winged grasshopper adult

LICHEN KATYDID

Katydids comprise a diverse group of insects and are particularly well adapted to survival in rainforests because of their exceptional camouflage. Most are nocturnal and extremely difficult to find. At night they come out of their hiding places to feed, sing, and mate. There are probably more than 150 species in Costa Rica, and a total of 162 species are known in Panama. The large number of species, their abundance in many habitats, and their lack of chemical defenses make them an important food for lizards, birds, bats, monkeys, frogs, spiders, mantises, army ants, and other invertebrates.

Markia hystrix
Length: 2.2 inches.
Range: Costa Rica and Panama.
Elevational range: Lowlands to at least 4,500 feet.

Most katydids are well camouflaged with brown or leaf-like green markings. The Lichen katydid, however, has one of the most incredible camouflages of all. It resembles the pale greenish-white lichens on which it lives in rainforest treetops. Not only does the color match the lichens but the body and legs also have a bizarre assortment of spines and points that blend well with lichens. This is an extraordinary example of how the processes of natural selection over thousands of years have resulted in camouflage colors and structures that match the katydid's habitat so well that the insect is extremely difficult for predators to find.

This nocturnal katydid eats flower parts and young leaves and is capable of flights shorter than 100 feet. It appears to be more common in moist and wet forests at middle elevations of the Caribbean slope and the southern Pacific slope. The best chance to see the Lichen Katydid is where lights are turned on at night with an adjacent sheet to attract nocturnal insects in the rainforest. The specimen shown here was attracted to a night light at Rancho Naturalista.

Lichen katydid, showing remarkable camouflage

LEAF-MIMIC KATYDID

Mimetica spp.
Length: 1.3–1.4 inches.
Range: Belize to Brazil.
Elevational range: Sea level to 3,900 feet.

Leaf-mimic katydid, looking like a dead leaf

Leaf-mimic katydid close-up

The Leaf-mimic katydids are among those extremely well camouflaged insects that exemplify the incredible adaptations of insects to avoid predation in the rainforest. These katydids have wing coverts that resemble dead leaves to such a fine level of detail that even the veins of the leaves are apparent. Some of them are brown to resemble dead leaves, some are green to resemble live leaves, and others are green with brown splotches that resemble leaves with damage. These nocturnal insects are known to align their leaflike bodies with existing leaves to make it more difficult for predators to spot them.

This remarkable camouflage helps explain a couple of types of bird behavior in the rainforest. An insect-eating bird in the rainforest would have a difficult time spotting edible insects like this katydid if it were hunting by itself. That is why it is not uncommon to encounter a mixed flock of tanagers, antbirds, warblers, and other species hunting as a group, because they are more effective in flushing and capturing these well-camouflaged insects.

For similar reasons, many different birds, ranging from tinamous to antbirds, follow swarms of army ants. Army ants are thorough in flushing any well-hidden insects during their raids. This exposes the insects as they try to escape and makes them vulnerable to being caught and eaten by the ant-following birds.

In another behavioral adaptation by many tropical birds to such well-camouflaged insects, offspring will stay with their parents for a year after hatching. They help forage for insects to feed the nestlings in the following year. Since the rainforest insects are so hard to spot, the two parents apparently have a difficult time finding enough insects to feed their young. When the yearlings help out, it greatly increases the chances for the young birds to survive.

Little is known about the life history of this katydid. It can be encountered at night lights at rainforest lodges and research field stations at lowland and middle elevations of the Caribbean slope. The specimen shown here was photographed at the night light at Rancho Naturalista near Turrialba.

CONEHEAD KATYDID (GIANT SPEARBEARER)

This distinctive rainforest katydid is known for the prominent horn on the top of its head that gives it the specific
name "rhinoceros." Like other katydids, this is a herbivo-
rous insect that forages on plants and is seldom observed
because it occurs in the rainforest canopy. This nocturnal
species may be best encountered at night lights at rainforest lodges or research centers.

This species occurs at lowland and middle elevations
of the Caribbean slope and at middle elevations of the
southern Pacific slope. The specimen shown here was
observed at the night light at Rancho Naturalista near
Turrialba.

Copiphora rhinoceros
Length: 1.5–1.6 inches.
Range: Nicaragua and Costa Rica.
Elevational range: Sea level to
 4,500 feet.

Conehead katydid

HOODED MANTIS

Choeradodis rhomboidea
Length: 2.2–2.6 inches.
Range: Mexico to South America.
Elevational range: Sea level to
3,600 feet.

This is one of those remarkable insects that shows extreme camouflage. The round green thorax and leafy-green wing coverts allow this large mantis to blend into surrounding vegetation as it awaits small invertebrate prey. The wing coverts not only display venation patterns of leaves but some also have brown splotches that resemble a damaged leaf. This makes it extremely hard for predators like birds or monkeys to spot them.

This genus is found in tropical environments of India as well as in tropical regions of Latin America from southern Mexico to central South America.

A close-up view of this mantis as it raises its head and thorax gives a classic view of an insect that approaches the image of an alien creature. The best place to look for it is along the Caribbean coastal lowlands from Tortuguero NP southward to the Cahuita area. The author has encountered this species twice in the courtyard of Tortuga Lodge. It also occurs on the Osa Peninsula and in the southern Pacific lowlands.

Hooded mantis camouflaged on a leaf

Hooded mantis, rearing up to attack its prey

TERMITES

Termites are a conspicuous component of Costa Rica's insect fauna. They play an important role in recycling wood fibers from trees, they provide a food source for mammals like tamanduas, and their arboreal nests provide important nesting sites for birds like parakeets, puffbirds, and trogons. They are also of economic importance because of the damage they can do to wooden structures like houses, telephone poles, and fence posts. That is why visitors in Costa Rica will often see concrete telephone and power poles and houses on stilts. The concrete poles are termite-proof, and the stilts can be treated to keep termites from reaching the house and damaging the boards in the home.

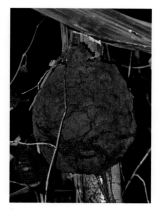
Termite colony on a young tree

Nasutitermes spp.
Costa Rican names: *Comején; hormiga blanca.*
Length: 0.2–0.6 inch.
Range: Central America.
Elevational range: Sea level to at least 3,600 feet.

The large oval, dark brown to grayish termite colonies are about 14 to 20 inches long. They are frequently seen atop roadside fence posts, on the sides of trees, and straddling tree branches throughout much of the lowlands in Costa Rica in dry, moist, and wet forests. Worker termites make the nests by chewing up wood fibers and bonding them with a fecal juice. This provides a relatively secure and waterproof colony site for the termites. Colonies consist of blind workers, soldiers, and a king and a queen termite. The soldiers, called nasutes, use chemical warfare to defend their colony. The large head of the nasute is designed as a squirt gun adapted for squirting a noxious sticky juice at creatures that invade the colony. The juice smells like turpentine and tends to discourage invasions by mammals like tamanduas and is a powerful deterrent to insect predators. Other chemicals called pheromones are used by the blind workers to follow trails that lead to their food supplies.

Termites are eaten by tamanduas, *Norops* lizards, and some other insects. It is always worth taking a second look at termite colonies on trees and fence posts to see if there is a hole, perhaps two or three inches in diameter, on the bottom or side. That would be the entrance hole made by parakeets, trogons, or puffbirds for access to the inside of the nest so they can use it for nesting. This provides a secure and waterproof location for them to incubate their eggs.

Termite colony showing a hole on the side, excavated for use as a bird nest

LANTERN BUG FAMILY *(Fulgoridae)*

PEANUT-HEAD BUG

*Fulgora laternaria and Fulgora
lampetis*
Costa Rican name: *Machaca*
Length: 3 inches.
Range: Mexico to central South
America.
Elevational range: Sea level to
about 1,200 feet.

Peanut-head bug compared with caiman
head. Bug photo by Dan Janzen.

The famous machacas are tropical insects associated with
a host of folklore and gee-whiz facts. In spite of their
imposing size, they are harmless. Nevertheless, local people in Latin America have long recounted the folktale that
if a girl is stung by a machaca, she must go to bed with her
boyfriend within twenty-four hours or she will die.

Another local name for this insect is "peanut-head bug"
because of the large, hollow structure on the front of the
head that superficially looks like a peanut. Closer examina-
tion reveals a remarkable likeness to a caiman head. Perhaps this mimicry of a ferocious reptile discourages birds
or other potential predators from attacking the insect. The
eyes of the machaca are actually at the rear of the false
head. If the false head does not deter an attacker, the bug
has another defense. It opens its wings to expose large eyespots on each hindwing, resembling the eyes of a large bird
like an owl. That should serve to scare away more potential predators. If that doesn't work, the machaca can also
spray a skunky-smelling fluid into the air as it flies from its
attacker. Normally, however, the insect's cryptic markings
make it difficult for predators to spot the machaca as it
rests during the day on the trunks of tropical trees.

Machacas occur in both tropical dry, moist, and wet
forests. *Fulgora laternaria* is found mainly in the dry
forests of the Guanacaste province and in the northwestern Caribbean lowlands in the vicinity of Caño Negro
NWR. *F. lampetis* is found in Guanacaste as well as in the
Caribbean and southern Pacific lowlands. They will come
to night lights. In Guanacaste they are most frequently
encountered resting on the trunks of guapinol trees
(*Hymenaea courbaril*).

Peanut-head bug with wings outspread,
showing eyespots. Photo by Dan Janzen.

Peanut-head bug (machaca). Photo by Dan Janzen.

DOBSON FLY

The ferocious-looking pincers of male dobson flies make them appear quite intimidating. The huge pincers are used for dueling among males during battles for females and for prodding the females during subsequent courtship rituals. The females lack large pincers. Adults do not feed, and they live for only one or two weeks.

Dobson flies are extremely adaptable insects, as evidenced by their occurrence throughout much of the temperate and tropical regions of North and South America. Their larval form is perhaps better known than the adults. Larvae are called hellgrammites and are a voracious aquatic predator in ponds and streams. In some areas hellgrammites are popular as fish bait.

Females lay masses of 300 to 3,000 eggs near water. The aggressive larvae prey on small invertebrates, fishes, and amphibians. In northern regions, the life cycle of the dobson fly is one to five years, but the length of the life cycle is not known in tropical regions. This species occurs primarily along streams and is rarely encountered except when attracted to lights at night. At such lights, like those at Rancho Naturalista, it is possible to examine the impressive design of these conspicuous insects.

Corydalus spp.
Length: 2.8–6.3 inches.
Range: Southern Canada to Brazil.
Elevational range: Sea level to at least 5,000 feet.

Dobson fly male with pincers

HARLEQUIN BEETLE

Acrocinus longimanus
Costa Rican name: *Arlequín.*
Length: 3 inches, excluding
   antennae.
Range: Southern Mexico to Brazil.
Elevational range: Sea level to
   3,600 feet.

The Harlequin is one of the most distinctive beetles of the lowland rainforest. Named for its harlequin color pattern, it is also distinguished by antennae over four inches long. This beetle can utilize several trees as host plants for egg laying, including strangler fig (*Ficus*), *Lonchocarpus, Artocarpus, Guazuma, Chorisia, Enterolobium, Urostigma, Castilla, Chlorophora, Brosimum,* and *Parahancornia.*

Adults are most active during the rainy season (July–September). Females usually select trees that have a bracket fungus. The markings of the fungus provide camouflage for the beetles and perhaps are characteristic of wood that is at the right point of decay to provide good habitat for the larvae. Each female lays fifteen to twenty eggs. It takes about twelve months from the time eggs are laid until adults emerge. Adults can be attracted to lights at night and also to dripping sap at tree wounds. They are especially attracted to the sap of *Bagassa guianensis.* In an interesting example of commensalism (meaning that both species involved in this relationship benefit from their interaction), pseudoscorpions are frequently found living under the wing covers (elytra) of this beetle.

Harlequin beetle at night light, showing long antennae

Harlequin beetle camouflaged on a log

HERCULES BEETLE

The impressive Hercules beetle is distinguished by a body that is almost 1.5 inches wide and 5 inches long, including a huge horn on the males. The horn on this beetle curves downward, unlike the horn on the similar-sized Rhinoceros beetle, which curves upward. Although not common, it is one of the most imposing insects of the American tropics.

This beetle is reported to be the strongest creature on Earth for its size. It can supposedly carry 850 times its body weight. This strength is put to the test when males battle each other for rights to mate with a female.

A species of middle elevations, it lives in moist and wet forests and cloud forests, where the larvae develop in the rotting trunks of fallen trees. The enormous larva takes about two years to develop into a beetle. Reaching a length of 4.1 inches, it weighs nearly a quarter pound. Adult beetles are mainly nocturnal, but they are sometimes encountered at dawn and dusk. They can be attracted to lights at night, particularly during the rainy season (July–September). They have been observed at Tortuga Lodge and at Rancho Naturalista.

Dynastes hercules septentrionalis
Costa Rican name: *Cornizuelo.*
Length: 2.1–5.9 inches.
Range: *D. hercules,* Mexico to Bolivia and Brazil; subspecies, Mexico to Panama.
Elevational range: 2,600–6,600 feet.

Hercules beetle male

RHINOCEROS BEETLE

Megasoma occidentalis (formerly Megasoma elephas occidentalis)
Costa Rican name: *Cornizuelo.*
Length: 2.1–3.2 inches.
Range: Southern Mexico to Venezuela.
Elevational range: Sea level to 3,000 feet.

This is one of the classic rainforest insects, a real show-stopper for natural-history enthusiasts. It is over three inches long, and the male has an imposing rhinoceros-like horn that it uses for fighting with other males when they compete for mates or for feeding sites. The female is also large but lacks the large horn. The only other large horned beetle in Costa Rica is *Dynastes hercules,* but that beetle is easily distinguished by the downward curve of its horn.

This beetle has a long life span, which is spent mainly in the larval form in enormous logs that lie on the floor of the rainforest. A larva takes from three to four years to develop into a pupa and then hatch into a beetle. Because of the habitat niche occupied by this beetle, it needs undisturbed lowland rainforest where large trees can fall and decay without being removed for their lumber. Costa Rica's lowland rainforest reserves like Tortuguero National Park help provide the habitat needs of this remarkable beetle.

In some areas of the Caribbean lowlands, people can be seen selling these live beetles along the roadside for use as pets; there are currently no laws prohibiting their possession and sale. It is not known if such prac-tices are detrimental to the status of Rhinoceros Beetle populations.

Rhinoceros beetle male

GOLDEN BEETLE

The stunning Golden beetle looks like it has been gold-plated. A species of middle to high elevations, it occurs in both wet forests and coffee plantations. Although the golden coloration may seen very conspicuous, the mirror-like surface of the beetle reflects the subdued green colors of its surrounding vegetation and camouflages it very well.

There are seventy-eight members of the genus *Chrysina* in the American tropics, and twenty-two of those are known from Costa Rica. Many members of this genus occur at higher elevations because host plants include oaks (*Quercus*) and alder (*Alnus*). In spite of this beetle's beauty, details of the life history are poorly known. Adults are seldom seen in the forest because they spend much of their life in the canopy, but the females fly down from the forest canopy to lay eggs in partially rotten tree trunks, where the larvae then feed on decomposing wood. The length of time from egg laying to emergence from the pupa is approximately one year.

This beetle is most apparent when it is attracted to night lights early in the rainy season (May and June). Most records for *Chrysina resplendens* are from mountains of the Monteverde area, Volcano Arenal, montane forests and coffee plantations in the vicinity of the Poás and Barva volcanoes, and northern regions of the Talamanca mountain range.

Chrysina resplendens (formerly Plusiotis resplendens)
Length: 0.8–0.9 inch.
Range: Costa Rica and Panama.
Elevational range: 1,300–9,200 feet.

Golden beetle

STINGLESS BEES

Trigona spp.
Costa Rican names: *Abeja atarrá; abeja jicote.*
Length: 0.2–0.3 inches.
Range: Southern Mexico to Brazil.
Elevational range: Sea level to 5,100 feet.

Stingless bees are inconspicuous insects of tropical forests until you learn how to spot their colonies. They build a faucetlike tube that sticks out perpendicular to the trunks of large trees, usually about one to six feet above the ground. These tubes are usually four to six inches long and may be straight or turn down at an angle that prevents rain from entering. Each colony of stingless bees contains three to ten thousand individuals and is safely located within a hollow tree or in subterranean cavities among the roots of a tree. Stingless bee colonies inhabit the dry forests of Guanacaste and moist and wet forests of the Caribbean lowlands and the southern Pacific lowlands. The bee *Trigona fulviventris* is among the most common and widespread of sixty stingless bee species in Costa Rica. Each colony defends a territory with an average radius of 300 feet and collects pollen and nectar from a wide variety of flowers within that area.

Although this bee is harmless and has no stinger, it can create a disturbing problem. Its attack pheromone is citronella, so if you use shampoo with a citronella base while visiting in a tropical forest, stingless bees may become entangled in your hair.

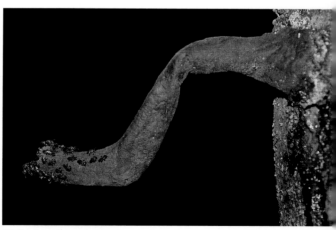

Stingless bee colony entrance

LEAFCUTTER ANT

Leafcutter ants are among the best-known rainforest insects. Their trails, four to six inches wide, are conspicuous on the forest floor because the ground looks like it has been cleaned with a vacuum. The ants form a continuous procession as worker ants carry circular portions of leaves back to the colony. All daughters of the queen, they are called media workers. Sometimes aggressive little minima workers ride on the leaf portions. As bodyguards, they protect the media workers from parasitic flies in the family Phoridae. These flies attempt to lay eggs on the neck of the media worker. If successful, the fly larva burrows into the ant's head and kills the ant. The ant colonies are also protected by large soldier ants that are over three-fourths of an inch long.

Once the ant reaches the underground nest, the leaf portions are cleaned and chewed into tiny portions. Saliva and ant fecal material, which contain enzymes that help break down the leaf, are then added. Tiny portions of a special fungus are also added so that the leaf creates a substrate for the growth of the fungus. These ants cannot eat or digest the leaves directly. Instead, they eat the fungus, which grows only in the colonies of leafcutter ants and is an example of symbiosis. Within the chambers of the colony, the fungus gardens grow into a spongy globular mass that may be six to twelve inches in diameter.

One colony may contain as many as five million ants and a queen that may live from seven to twenty years. The colony is apparent on the surface of the ground because many ant trails converge at a large mound of dirt, leaf litter, dead ants, and other debris. One mound was estimated to contain almost thirty cubic yards of soil and organic material that were brought to the surface over a period of six and a half years. Because of this excavation practice, leafcutters are important in recycling treetop nutrients. The nutrients become available to other organisms after use by the ants.

Leafcutter ants can be seen at most forest reserves and national parks in the Caribbean and Pacific lowlands, including Tortuguero NP, Tortuga Lodge, La Selva Biological Field Station, Monteverde, Las Baulas NP near Tamarindo, Palo Verde NP, Santa Rosa NP, Guanacaste NP, lower levels of Braulio Carrillo NP, Rancho Naturalista, Corcovado NP, and Tiskita Jungle Lodge.

Atta cephalotes
Costa Rican name: *Zompopas.*
Length: 0.08–0.8 inches.
Range: Southern Mexico to Northern Argentina.
Elevational range: Sea level to 6,600 feet.

Leafcutter ants carrying leaf parts

Leafcutter ant close-up

AZTECA ANTS

Azteca spp.
Length: 0.2–0.3 inch.
Range: Mexico to Argentina
Elevational range: Sea level to 3,900 feet.

Like Army ants and Leafcutter ants, Azteca ants are among the best-known of rainforest species in the American tropics. These ants, which include a number of species in the same genus, are also called cecropia ants, because one of the most common locations for their colonies is in natural cavities in the trunks of cecropia trees. Among the species found in Costa Rica are *Azteca xanthochroa, A. constrictor, A. ovaticeps, A. coeruleipennis,* and *A. instabilis.* Since cecropia is an early successional tree that grows in tropical lowlands wherever there are openings in the forest, the ants have an abundance of potential habitat. The ants will also make their colonies in trees of *Cordia, Terminalia, Cocoloba, Triplaris,* and *Pithecellobium.*

Azteca ants are aggressive against other ants that try to establish colonies near them. They attack the colonies and drive the other species away. Within their own colony, they are ant farmers. They manage colonies of mealybugs, tiny insects in the family Pseudococcidae. The ants eat the sugary juices produced in the mealybugs and then extruded from them.

Predators of Azteca ants include some of Costa Rica's larger woodpeckers, including the Chestnut-colored Woodpecker, Lineated Woodpecker, and Pale-billed Woodpecker. They are large enough to open the trunks of these trees easily and expose the ants and larvae.

Azteca ants on cecropia

Azteca ants on cecropia stem

BULLET ANT

The notorious Bullet ant is the largest ant in Central America. This large black ant is a solitary hunter found only in the Caribbean lowlands. It is especially common at La Selva Biological Field Station and should be looked for on tree trunks and trail-marker pipes during hikes in the Arboretum area. This ant should be avoided because it can give an extremely painful sting, the source of the ant's Costa Rican name, *bala,* meaning "bullet." Although individuals can be encountered during the daytime, this species hunts smaller insect prey mainly at night. It hunts from ground level up to the canopy.

Bullet ant profile; hand is for scale.

Nests of this ant are made of complex subterranean tunnels and chambers with an entrance hole at the base of large trees like *Pentaclethra macroloba.* The oval entrance holes are about 0.8 inch wide by 2.4 inches high. Each colony contains from 700 to 1,400 worker ants that hunt for the colony.

Paraponera clavata
Costa Rican name: *Bala.*
Length: 0.6–0.9 inches.
Range: Nicaragua to Brazil.
Elevational range: Sea level to 1,600 feet.

Bullet ant

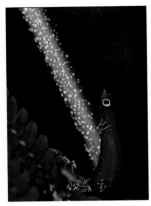

Bullhorn acacia ants; hole on thorn is the colony entrance

Pseudomyrmex spp.
Costa Rican name: *Hormiga de cornizuelo.*
Length: 0.2 inch.
Range: Southern Mexico to Colombia.
Elevational range: Sea level to 4,000 feet.

BULLHORN ACACIA ANTS

Bullhorn acacia ants demonstrate symbiosis (mutualism) in the form of the mutually beneficial relationship that exists between them and the bullhorn acacia shrubs that provide their home. The bullhorn acacia (*Acacia* spp.) includes several species of short, thorny shrubs in the Pacific lowlands and middle elevations, including the Central Plateau. It is most abundant in the tropical dry forests of Guanacaste and can be seen in Palo Verde, Santa Rosa, and Guanacaste NPs; Lomas Barbudal Biological Reserve; La Pacífica; Hacienda Solimar; La Ensenada Lodge; and south to Carara and Corcovado NPs.

The shrub has large paired hollow thorns that look like bull horns, from which the plant gets its name. New growth has small circular nectaries on the top side of the leaf petioles that provide nectar for the ants. At the tips of new leaflets are circular brown structures called Beltian bodies that provide a nutritious protein diet for the ants. The hollow horns provide a home for the ants, which chew an entry hole into the horn at the tip. All of these features have developed through natural selection to accommodate the ants' basic needs for survival. One shrub can support one colony, which includes one queen, 10,000 to 15,000 worker ants, 2,000 males, 1,000 virgin queens, and up to 50,000 larvae. The queen may live twenty years.

Mutualism is the process whereby two species mutually benefit each other's survival. In this case, the ants benefit from the special features of the acacia, and in return they protect the plant from animals that might eat the stems or leaves. Whenever an animal tries to climb the shrub or lands on its branches, it is attacked and stung by the ants. The ants also kill other plants that sprout within four to six feet of the base of the shrub by cutting off new sprouts so the acacia does not have to compete for sunlight or for nutrients in the soil. However, orioles, Great Kiskadees, Yellow-olive Flycatchers, and Rufous-naped Wrens build nests on these shrubs. The ants tolerate them and protect the birds' nests.

Bare area under acacia tree cleared by acacia ants

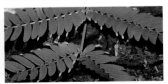

Protein bodies on acacia serve as food for acacia ants.

ARMY ANT

Army ants are well known for their legendary raids in which tens of thousands of ants spread across the forest floor in a fan-shaped column to capture whatever small living creatures are unable to escape. Collectively, Army ants include about 150 tropical species of ants, but the best-known is *Eciton burchelli.* These ants occur in colonies that may include from thirty thousand to more than a million individuals. Each colony contains one queen. The colonies include different castes of ants. Each caste has different duties. The most conspicuous and largest are soldier ants, which have large pincer mandibles. The males are the only caste with wings.

Army ants killing a cockroach

Army ants eat other ants, wasps, cockroaches, katydids, crickets, and other arthropods. The headquarters of a colony is known as a bivouac. It is formed from a solid mass of ants that link their bodies together with their feet into a living structure that conceals the queen, eggs, and larvae. Army ants begin raids early in the morning and form a fan-shaped column that may be ten to fifty feet wide.

Many creatures follow ant swarms and capture invertebrates flushed by the ants: Great Tinamous; Bicolored, Chestnut-backed, Immaculate, Ocellated, and Spotted Antbirds; Black-crowned Antpittas; Barred and Slaty Antshrikes; Black-faced Antthrushes; Barred, Plain-brown, Ruddy, and Tawny-winged Woodcreepers; Roadside Hawks; Cattle Egrets; Blue-crowned Motmots; Summer Tanagers; Squirrel Cuckoos; Buff-throated Saltators; and Ruddy Foliage-gleaners.

Parasitic flies follow the ants to lay eggs or larvae on escaping insects. Barred Forest-Falcons follow the swarm to prey on antbirds and woodcreepers. *Melinaea ethra* butterflies follow Army ant swarms in search of antbird droppings, because the females need to feed on the amino acids of the droppings so their eggs can develop. Other insects that accompany ant swarms are mites, silverfish, beetles, flies, and wasps. Some prey on the ants, and others live in mutualistic relationships with the ants.

Army ant swarms may be encountered in many Caribbean and Pacific lowland and middle-elevation sites, including dry forest reserves in Guanacaste, cloud forests at Monteverde, Corcovado Lodge Tent Camp and Corcovado NP on the Osa Peninsula, Tapantí NP, Wilson Botanical Garden, and Rancho Naturalista near Turrialba.

Eciton burchelli
Costa Rican name: *Hormiga arriera.*
Length: 0.1–0.6 inch.
Range: Southern United States to northern Argentina.
Elevational range: Sea level to 6,500 feet.

ORDER ARANEAE

Nephila clavipes
Costa Rican name: *Araña de oro.*
Length: 0.2–2.5 inches, including
   legs.
Range: South Florida and Texas to
   Panama.
Elevational range: Sea level to
   3,000 feet.

GOLDEN ORB-WEAVER

The Golden Orb-weaver is one of the largest spiders in Central America and is the largest orb-weaving spider in the New World. The females have bodies about one inch long, and when the legs are included, they average over 2.5 inches long. In contrast, the tiny males do not exceed a quarter inch in length, including the legs. When you encounter one of these spider webs, look carefully in an area within several inches of the conspicuous female. You will discover a tiny spider nearby, which is the male. The large webs of this spider may be up to two feet across and are distinguished by very strong golden yellow silk. This silk has tremendous strength, considering its diameter, and it has been used for industrial purposes like crosshairs in telescopes.

This spider is found in forest openings, along trails, and in second-growth forest areas where there is enough sunlight reaching the forest floor to provide good habitat for many second-growth insects that serve as prey. Webs are usually within several feet of the ground. This spider is found in lowland forests of both the Caribbean and Pacific slopes. Golden Orb-weavers prey on flies, beetles, moths, and butterflies. Once an insect is caught in the web, the spider bites it with venom that has digestive enzymes. The victim is wrapped in silk and taken back to the hub of the web, where the spider eats it. Some small spiders, wasps, damselflies, and hummingbirds routinely steal prey from the webs of these spiders.

Golden Orb-weaver, killing a Caligo
butterfly

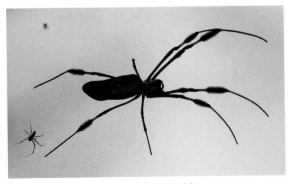

Golden Orb-weaver, female in center, male at lower left

LARGE FOREST-FLOOR MILLIPEDE

The Large Forest-floor millipede lives up to its name: it can be up to four inches long and is conspicuous on the rainforest floor. This millipede is typically found in moist and wet forest lowlands of the Caribbean slope, like along the foot trails of La Selva. The ecological function of this millipede is that it eats rotting wood and thereby recycles the nutrients of dead or fallen trees.

These millipedes are almost always encountered in pairs, with the male riding on top of the female. This is because of a very complex reproductive situation in which the females are receptive for extended periods of the year and will store sperm from males until the eggs are laid. Upon mating with the female, the male continues to ride atop the female to prevent other males from mating with her. If he departs, another male will soon take his place, and the chances of the original male passing on his genes declines.

One other unusual feature of this millipede protects it from predation. When confronted, it will roll up in a ball and can spray a toxic juice containing hydrogen cyanide and benzaldehyde on its attacker, as far as twelve inches away. More chemical warfare in the rainforest.

ORDER POLYDESMIDA

Nyssodesmus python
Costa Rican name: *Milpies.*
Size: 2.6–3.9 inches.
Range: Caribbean slope of Costa Rica.
Elevational range: Approximately sea level to 1,200 feet.

Large Forest-floor millipede, newly molted

Large Forest-floor millipede pair

ORDER DECAPODA

SALLY LIGHTFOOT CRAB

Grapsus grapsus
Costa Rican name: *Cangrejo.*
Carapace length: 3.25 inches.
Range: Florida to Brazil; Mexico to
Peru; Galápagos Islands.
Elevational range: Sea level.

The widespread Sally Lightfoot crab is a type of rock runner that is seen on both Pacific and Caribbean beaches. The carapace, round and flattened, is purplish brown with fine cream-colored spots. This active crab frequents rocky shorelines and beaches at and above the spray line.

Sally Lightfoot crab

MOUTHLESS CRAB (JACK-O-LANTERN CRAB)

The colorful Mouthless crab is found along the length of
the Pacific coast and leaves little doubt about its identity.
It has a black carapace, orange legs, and purple chelipeds
(front claw-bearing legs). The name "Jack-o-Lantern
Crab" comes from the facelike pattern of three yellow
spots on the front of the crab. One is between the eye
stalks, and the others are above and outside the eyestalks.
A nocturnal species, this crab can be observed with flash-
lights by walking the beach and nearby forests at night. It
forages on the sand and in adjacent upland mangrove forests and underbrush. It is common in the Tamarindo area
near the beaches used by nesting Leatherback Turtles and
along the beaches of Corcovado NP and Corcovado Lodge
Tent Camp on the Osa Peninsula.

Gecarcinus quadratus
Costa Rican name: *Cangrejo.*
Carapace length: 2 inches.
Range: Mexico to northwestern
  South America.
Elevational range: Sea level.

Mouthless crab

GLOSSARY

Abdomen: An insect has three main body parts, the head, thorax, and abdomen. The abdomen is the posterior portion of an insect's body.

Antennae: Long sensory appendages on the head of an insect. They may be slender and pointed, clubbed, or feathery.

Arthropod: A member of the phylum arthropoda, including segmented invertebrates like insects, spiders, and crustaceans.

Batesian mimicry: A type of mimicry in which two species outwardly resemble each other but only one possesses a defense against predators. For instance, a butterfly may have a color pattern that resembles that of another species with foul-tasting, toxic chemicals that deter predation. The similar markings fool predators into avoiding the edible species.

BR: Biological Reserve.

Canopy: A layer within the overall structure of a forest. *Lower canopy* refers to shrub layer and short trees; *midcanopy* refers to middle levels of foliage and structure among trees; *upper canopy* refers to the foliage and vegetative structure in the tops of the trees; and *supercanopy* refers to trees like *Ceiba* that project above the upper canopy.

Caribbean slope: The northern and eastern portion of Costa Rica, from the continental divide in the mountains eastward to the lowlands, that drains toward the Caribbean.

Caste: A group of individuals within a colony of ants or termites that has a singular role or function. For example, soldier ants defend their colony from attacks by other ants or other creatures.

Chrysalis: The pupal stage of a butterfly undergoing metamorphosis.

Clubbed antennae: Antennae that are thick at the tip.

Clutch: The eggs laid in a single nest, usually by a single female. (After hatching, the young are collectively referred to as a brood.)

Color morph: A color variety within a species, either adult or caterpillar, that deviates from normal coloration. Some morphs may be lighter or darker than the normal color.

Commensalism: A type of symbiosis in which both species involved in the relationship benefit from their interaction.

Cryptic: A type of coloration that makes a creature difficult to see because it blends in with the background.

Diurnal: Being active during daylight hours; opposite of nocturnal.

Dry forest: A forest in which the range of total annual rainfall is 40–80 inches per year. The dry forest in Costa Rica is found primarily in Guanacaste Province and is a tropical deciduous forest with distinct wet and dry seasons.

Dry season: That portion of the year in which less rainfall occurs. In Costa Rica, the dry season occurs from December through March and is most prevalent on the Pacific slope.

Elytra: An outer shell that protects the folded wings of a beetle. The beetle lifts them prior to taking flight.

Endemic: Occurring only within a limited geographic area and nowhere else in the world, such as species found only in the mountains of Costa Rica and western Panama, only in the lowlands of southeastern Costa Rica and adjacent Panama, or only on Cocos Island.

Foothills: Hilly terrain at the base of mountains with elevations of about 1,500–4,500 feet (approximately the same as the premontane or subtropical zone). The term is general, not ecologically based. The distribution of some species is limited to foothills and not to either lowlands or highlands.

Forewings: The front pair of wings on a moth or butterfly.

Gallery forest: A forest adjacent to a stream or river; also referred to as riparian forest.

Highlands: For the purposes of this book, regions at 5,000–11,000 feet in elevation, including moist, wet, and rainforests. They are characterized by 40–200 inches of rainfall per year. Such areas can have large numbers of epiphytes on the trees. The species diversity is less than at lower elevations. It includes 15 percent of Costa Rica's land area.

Hindwings: The rear pair of wings on a butterfly, moth, or other insect.

Host plant: The plant species that a butterfly or moth caterpillar eats prior to forming its cocoon. The adult typically lays its eggs on the host plant to ensure that the newly hatched caterpillars are exposed to the right food source.

Instar: One of five progressive stages in a caterpillar's development. A caterpillar typically goes through five instar stages before becoming a pupa. As the caterpillar grows through each instar, it must shed its skin by molting to allow increases in size.

Larva: Same as a caterpillar. After hatching from an egg, a caterpillar progresses through five instar stages while feeding on host plants and then forms a pupa (chrysalis) before emerging as an adult. This is called complete metamorphosis.

Lepidoptera: The taxonomic order that includes butterflies and moths within the class Insecta.

Lowlands: Relatively flat terrain between foothills and the coast, in the elevation range from sea level to about 2,000 feet. It includes dry, moist, and wet forests and accounts for 57 percent of Costa Rica's land area.

Mandible: Pincerlike mouthparts of an insect or arthropod that are used for eating, cutting, or chewing food.

Metamorphosis: The process by which a creature changes its form from an egg to a caterpillar into a cocoon (pupa) and then into a moth or butterfly, or from an egg to a tadpole to a frog.

Middle elevation: Elevations known as subtropical or premontane, including elevations of about 2,000 feet–4,500 feet; also referred to as foothills. This may include moist, wet, and rainforest habitats. The Central Plateau and San José are at middle elevations. This

zone includes 28 percent of Costa Rica's land area.

Migration: A regular two-way movement between wintering and summering areas or between breeding and nonbreeding areas.

Mimicry: The phenomenon by which one creature derives a survival advantage from its resemblance to another creature that has special defenses against predation. There are two main kinds of mimicry, Batesian and Müllerian.

Moist forest: A forest in tropical lowlands that receives 80–160 inches of rainfall per year. This type of forest covers 24 percent of Costa Rica's land area. At premontane and lower montane levels, moist forest receives 40–80 inches of rainfall and includes about 5 percent of Costa Rica's land area.

Montane forest: A highland wet forest (40–80 inches of rainfall per year) or rainforest (80–160 inches of rainfall per year) at 8,200–10,500 feet in elevation.

Müllerian mimicry: A type of mimicry in which two species, such as butterflies, share a characteristic that makes them undesirable to predators (e.g., odor or toxic chemicals). These qualities can make the predator very sick without killing it. Predators remember the markings of such creatures and avoid them, reducing predation on all species with those markings. The insects exemplifying Müllerian mimicry have similar identification marks that cause predators to avoid both species. A famous example is the pair of passionflower butterflies *Heliconius erato* and *H. melpomene.*

Mutualism: A symbiotic relationship between two species in which both species benefit from the relationship. An example is the relationship between acacia ants and the acacia tree.

Nectar: The sweet, sugary fluid that is secreted by the flowers of many plants. It is a primary food for many adult butterflies and moths.

Nocturnal: Active at night; the opposite of diurnal.

NP: National Park.

NWR: National Wildlife Refuge.

Nymph: The aquatic larva of a dragonfly. This is the intermediate stage of insects that have incomplete metamorphosis. They hatch from an egg into a nymph, and the nymph eventually emerges as an adult.

Ocellus (plural ocelli): Markings that look like eyeballs, on the wings of butterflies, moths, and other insects. They serve to surprise and disrupt attacks by birds.

Odonata: The order of dragonflies and damselflies within the class Insecta.

Pacific slope: That portion of the Costa Rican landscape that drains from the mountains west and south to the Pacific Ocean.

Paramo: A highland elevational zone above the montane zone, ranging from about 10,500 feet to the peaks of Costa Rica's mountains. The zone is above tree line and is characterized by stunted shrubs, bamboo, and many composites. It includes 0.2 percent of the country's land area.

Parataxonomist: A citizen who develops professional biological expertise through training and practical field experience in the collection and identification of specimens for scientific study.

Pheromone: Sexual attractant chemicals produced by some butterflies and moths to attract a mate.

Premontane: The elevational zone between approximately 2,000 and 4,900 feet; also referred to as foothills, subtropical, or middle elevations. The zone includes moist forests, wet forests, and rainforests at those elevations.

Primary forest: A mature forest that has not been cut in recent times.

Proboscis: The tubelike extensible tongue of a moth or butterfly that can be uncoiled in order to take in nectar, moisture, sap, or mineral-filled moisture from mud puddles, sand, or animal urine or droppings.

Pupa: The third stage in the life cycle of a butterfly or moth characterized by development within a shell-like chrysalis. The stage is preceded by the larva and followed by emergence as an adult.

Race: A genetically distinctive population within a species; may be differentiated by host plants, appearance, or geographic range.

Rainforest: A forest that receives more than 320

inches of rainfall per year. The term may also be used more generally to describe moist or wet forests.

Rainy season: That portion of the year in which most rain falls. In Costa Rica, this is the period from April to December.

Riparian forest: A forest along a stream or river; also referred to as gallery forest.

Secondary forest: A forest that has grown back after a previous disturbance, such as burning or cutting.

Species: A group of individuals or populations that are similar in structure, appearance, and physiology and that are capable of interbreeding and producing fertile offspring.

Subspecies: A subgroup or population within a species that is distinguished by similarity of host plants, genetics, markings, behavior, or geographic distribution.

Symbiosis: The interdependent relationship between two species in which each species benefits from the presence and lifestyle of the other.

Taxonomist: A person who specializes in the classification and naming of species.

Termitary: A nest of termites, usually located on a tree or fence post. Some birds like trogons and parakeets excavate their nest within a termitary.

Terrestrial: Living on the ground.

Thorax: An insect has three main body parts, the head, thorax, and abdomen. The thorax is the section behind the head, and the legs and wings are attached to it.

Tico: A person from Costa Rica.

Understory: Smaller trees, shrubs, and other vegetation that are generally less than 25 feet in height within a taller forest.

Urticating hairs: Spinelike hairs on the body of a moth or butterfly caterpillar that create an extremely irritating response if a creature tries to grab or eat the caterpillar.

Wet season: The season when most rainfall occurs in an area. Same as rainy season. In Costa Rica, this generally includes the period from April to December. In some areas, like the northeastern Caribbean lowlands, the wet season extends through most of the year.

BIBLIOGRAPHY

Aiello, Annette. 1992. Dry Season Strategies of Two Panamanian Butterfly Species, *Anartia fatima* (Nymphalinae) and *Pierella luna luna* (Satyrinae). In *Insects of Panama and Mesoamerica: Selected Studies,* ed. Diomedes Quintero and Annette Aiello, 573–575. New York: Oxford Univ. Press. 692 pp.

Ayensu, Edward S. 1980. *The Life and Mysteries of the Jungle.* New York: Crescent Books. 200 pp.

Brower, Lincoln P. 1983. Chemical Defense in Butterflies. In *Coevolution,* ed. Douglas J. Futuyma and Montgomery Slatkin, 109–134. Sunderland, Mass.: Sinauer Assoc. 555 pp.

Carroll, C. R. 1983. *Azteca* (Hormega Azteca, Azteca Ants, Cecropia Ants). In *Costa Rican Natural History,* ed. Daniel H. Janzen, 691–693. Chicago: Univ. of Chicago Press. 816 pp.

Carter, David. 1992. *Butterflies and Moths.* Eyewitness Handbooks. New York: Dorling Kindersley. 304 pp.

Chacón, Isidro, and José Montero. 2007. *Butterflies and Moths of Costa Rica.* Heredia, Costa Rica: Instituto Nacional de Biodiversidad. 366 pp.

Corrales, Jorge F. 1996. *Las mariposas* Heliconius *de Costa Rica.* Heredia, Costa Rica: Instituto Nacional de Biodiversidad. Booklet. 34 pp.

———. 1999. *Mariposas comunes, Area de Conservación Tempisque, Costa Rica.* Santo Domingo de Heredia: Instituto Nacional de Biodiversidad. 116 pp.

DeVries, Philip J. 1983. *Heliconius hecale.* In *Costa Rican Natural History,* ed. Daniel H. Janzen, 730–731. Chicago: Univ. of Chicago Press. 816 pp.

———. 1983. *Morpho peleides.* In *Costa Rican Natural History,* ed. Daniel H. Janzen, 741–742. Chicago: Univ. of Chicago Press. 816 pp.

———. 1987. *The Butterflies of Costa Rica and Their Natural History.* Vol. 1, *Papilionidae, Pieiridae, Nymphalidae.* Princeton, N.J.: Princeton Univ. Press. 327 pp.

———. 1997. *The Butterflies of Costa Rica and Their Natural History.* Vol. 2, *Riodinidae.* Princeton, N.J.: Princeton Univ. Press. 288 pp.

Emmons, Katherine M., Robert H. Horwich, James Kamstra, Ernesto Saqui, James Beveridge, Timothy McCarthy, Jan Meerman, Scott C. Silver, Ignacio Pop, Fred Koontz, Emiliano Pop, Hermelindo Saqui, Linde Ostro, Pedro Pixabaj, Dorothy Beveridge, and Judy Lumb. 1996. *Cockscomb Basin Wildlife Sanctuary: Its History, Flora, and Fauna.* Cay Caulker, Belize: Producciones de la Hamaca. 334 pp.

Fincke, Ola M. 1992. Behavioural Ecology of the Giant Damselflies of Barro Colorado Island, Panama. In *Insects of Panama and Mesoamerica: Selected Studies,* ed. Diomedes Quintero and Annette Aiello, 102–113. New York: Oxford Univ. Press. 692 pp.

Heisler, I. L. 1983. *Nyssodesmus python* (Milpies, Large Forest-floor Millipede). In *Costa Rican Natural History,* ed. Daniel H. Janzen, 747–748. Chicago: Univ. of Chicago Press. 816 pp.

Henry, Charles S., Norman D. Penny, and Phillip A. Adams. 1992. The Neuropteroid Orders of Central America (Neuroptera and Megaloptera). In *Insects of Panama and Mesoamerica: Selected Studies,* ed. Diomedes Quintero and Annette Aiello, 432–458. New York: Oxford Univ. Press. 692 pp.

Holland, W. J. 1968. *The Moth Book: A Guide*

to the Moths of North America. New York: Dover. 479 pp.

Horwich, Robert H., and Jonathan Lyon. 1990. *A Belizean Rain Forest: The Community Baboon Sanctuary.* Gays Mills, Wisc.: Orangutan Press. 420 pp.

Howden, H. F. 1983. *Megasoma elephas* (Cornizuelo, Rhinoceros Beetle). In *Costa Rican Natural History,* ed. Daniel H. Janzen, 735–736. Chicago: Univ. of Chicago Press. 816 pp.

Janzen, D. H., ed. 1983. *Costa Rican Natural History.* Chicago: Univ. of Chicago Press. 816 pp.

Janzen, D. H., and C. L. Hogue. 1983. *Fulgora laternaria* (Machaca, Peanut-head bug, Lantern Fly). In *Costa Rican Natural History,* ed. Daniel H. Janzen, 726–727. Chicago: Univ. of Chicago Press. 816 pp.

Kaplan, Eugene H. 1988. *Southeastern and Caribbean Seashores.* Peterson Field Guides. Boston: Houghton Mifflin. 425 pp.

Lemaire, Claude. 1988. *The Saturniidae of America: Ceratocampinae.* San José, Costa Rica: Museo Nacional de Costa Rica. 480 pp.

Lubin, Y. D. 1983. *Nasutitermes* (Comején, Hormiga Blanca, Nasute Termite, Arboreal Termite). In *Costa Rican Natural History,* ed. Daniel H. Janzen, 743–745. Chicago: Univ. of Chicago Press. 816 pp.

Miller, J. C., Daniel H. Janzen, and Winnie Hallwachs. 2006. One Hundred Caterpillars. Cambridge, Mass.: Harvard Univ. Press. 264 pp.

Monge-Najera, Julián. 1992. Clicking Butterflies, *Hamadryas,* of Panama: Their Biology and Identification. In *Insects of Panama and Mesoamerica,* ed. Diomedes Quintero and Annette Aiello, 567–572. New York: Oxford Univ. Press. 692 pp.

Morón, Miguel-Angel. 1990. *The Beetles of the World.* Vol. 10, *Rutelini, Part 1: Plusiotis, Chrysina, Chrysophora, Pelidnotopsis, Ectinoplectron.* Venette, France: Sciences Nat, Imprimerie de Compiègne. 280 pp.

———. 1997. *Atlas de los Escarabajos de México: Coleoptera: Lamellicornia.* Vol. 1, *Familia Melolonthidae: Subfamilias Rutelinae, Dynastinae, Cetoniinae, Trichiinae, Valginae, y Melolonthinae.* Mexico City: CONABIO. 145 pp.

Murawski, Darlyne A. 1993. A Taste for Poison. *National Geographic* 184(6): 122–137.

Nickle, David A. 1992. Katydids of Panama. In *Insects of Panama and Mesoamerica: Selected Studies,* ed. Diomedes Quintero and Annette Aiello, 142–184. New York: Oxford Univ. Press. 692 pp.

Norman, David. 1995. Moths Brighten Sky in Mysterious Migration. *Tico Times* 39(1335): 14. September 8.

Rowell, H. F. 1983. *Tropidacris cristata* (Saltamonte o Chapulín Gigante, Giant Red-winged Grasshopper). In *Costa Rican Natural History,* ed. Daniel H. Janzen, 772–773. Chicago: Univ. of Chicago Press. 816 pp.

Scott, James A. 1986. *The Butterflies of North America: A Natural History and Field Guide.* Stanford, Calif.: Stanford Univ. Press. 583 pp.

Silberglied, Robert. 1983. *Anartia fatima.* In *Costa Rican Natural History,* ed. Daniel H. Janzen, 682–683. Chicago: Univ. of Chicago Press. 816 pp.

Smith, Neal G. 1983. *Urania fulgens.* In *Costa Rican Natural History,* ed. Daniel H. Janzen, 775–776. Chicago: Univ. of Chicago Press. 816 pp.

———. 1992. Reproductive Behaviour and Ecology of *Urania* (Lepidoptera: Uraniidae) Moths and Their Larval Food Plants, *Omphalea* spp. In *Insects of Panama and Mesoamerica: Selected Studies,* ed. Diomedes Quintero and Annette Aiello, 576–593. New York: Oxford Univ. Press. 692 pp.

Solís, Angel. 1998. Los Escarabajos Dorados (*Plusiotis*) de Costa Rica. Santo Domingo de Heredia, Costa Rica: INBIO. 2 pp.

Stevens, George C. 1983. Leafcutter Ant (*Atta cephalotes*). In *Costa Rican Natural History,* ed. Daniel H. Janzen, 688–691. Chicago: Univ. of Chicago Press. 816 pp.

Stout, Jean. 1983. Helicopter Damselflies (*Megaloprepus* and *Mecistogaster*). In *Costa Rican Natural History,* ed. Daniel H. Janzen, 734–735. Chicago: Univ. of Chicago Press. 816 pp.

Struttman, Jane M. 1999. *Rothschildia lebeau: Moths of North America.* N. Prairie Wildlife Research Center, Jamestown, N.D.: U.S. Geological Survey, www.npwrc.usgs.gov/

resource/distr/depid/MOTHS/usa/1003. html.

Turner, John R. G. 1983. Mimicry: The Palatability Spectrum and Its Consequences. In *Coevolution,* ed. Douglas J. Futuyma and Montgomery Slatkin, 141–161. Sunderland, Mass.: Sinauer Assoc. 555 pp.

Tveten, John, and Gloria Tveten. 1996. *Butterflies of Houston and Southeast Texas.* Austin: Univ. of Texas Press. 292 pp.

Young, Allen M. 1991. *Sarapiquí Chronicle: A Naturalist in Costa Rica.* Washington, D.C.: Smithsonian Institution Press. 361 pp.

APPENDICES

APPENDIX A: COSTA RICAN CONSERVATION ORGANIZATIONS

Asociación Ornitológica de Costa Rica: Apdo 2289-1002, San José, Costa Rica. E-mail: contacto@avesdecostarica.org. Web site: www.avesdecostarica.org. Fax: 506-2278-1564.

Association for the Conservation of Nature (ASCONA): Apdo 83790-1000, San José, Costa Rica. Telephone: 506-2233-3188.

Birding Club of Costa Rica: Web newsletter *Tico Tweeter* reports on recent and upcoming birding trips and birding discoveries at various sites and lodges. E-mail: costaricabirding@hotmail.com.

Caribbean Conservation Corporation: Gainesville, Florida. Telephone: 1-800-678-7853. Web site: www.cccturtle.org.

Corcovado Foundation: A non-profit organization dedicated to protection of the rainforest and wildlife in Corcovado National Park, where there have been recent problems with poaching of endangered wildlife species. www.corcovadofoundation.org.

Costa Rica Birding Trail: A new effort in the northern region of Costa Rica to promote birding along a trail of lodges and protected areas that provide a stimulating variety of habitats. www.costaricanbirdroute.com.

Gone Birding: Information about birding and birding activities in Costa Rica, authored by expert birder Richard Garrigues. Google "gone birding newsletter."

Great Green Macaw Research and Conservation Project: Cooperative project headed by the Tropical Science Center and dedicated to the protection and restoration of the Great Green Macaw in the Caribbean lowlands of Costa Rica. www.lapaverde.or.cr/lapa.

Henderson Birding: www.hendersonbirding.com. The author's Web site, where updates, new information, and corrections to the *Field Guide to the Wildlife of Costa Rica* will be posted. Includes Costa Rica birding information, trip tips, preparation checklist, and itineraries for future birding trips.

La Selva Biological Field Station, OTS: Apdo 53-3069, Puerto Viejo de Sarapiquí, Heredia, Costa Rica. Telephone: 506-2766-6565; e-mail: laselva@sloth.ots.ac.cr.

Las Cruces Biological Station and Wilson Botanical Garden, OTS: Apdo 73, 8257 San Vito, Coto Brus, Costa Rica. Telephone: 506-2773-4004; e-mail: lcruces@hortus.ots.ac.cr.

Los Cusingos Neotropical Bird Sanctuary: The former home of Dr. Alexander Skutch, now managed by the Tropical Science Center. P.O. Box 8-3870-1000, San José, Costa Rica. Telephone: 506-2253-3276; e-mail: cecitrop@sol.racsa.co.cr.

Monteverde Conservation League: Apdo 10165-1000, San José, Costa Rica. Manages the Children's Eternal Rainforest. Telephone: 506-2645-5003; e-mail acmmcl@sol.racsa.co.cr. www.acmcr.org; also www.monteverdeinfo.com.

National Biodiversity Institute (INBIO): Apdo 22-3100, Santo Domingo, Heredia, Costa Rica. National organization dedicated to the creation of a comprehensive inventory of all of Costa Rica's plant and wildlife species; with biological collections now exceeding 3.5 million specimens and many excellent publications. Telephone: 506-2507-8100. www.inbio.ac.cr.

National Parks Foundation (Fundación de Parques Nacionales): Apdo 236-1002, San José, Costa Rica. Telephone: 506-2222-4921 or 506-2223-8437.

Organization for Tropical Studies, Inc.: North American Headquarters, Box 90630, Durham, NC 27708-0630. www.ots.duke.edu; also www.ots.ac.cr. Costa Rican office: Apdo 676, 2050 San Pedro do Montes de Oca, San José, Costa Rica. Telephone: 506-2240-6696; e-mail: oet@cro.ots.ac.cr.

Rainforest Action Network: 221 Pine Street, Suite 500, San Francisco, CA 94104. Telephone: 415-398-4404. www.ran.org.

Rincón Rainforest: A protected tropical forest of 13,838 acres in northern Costa Rica. Donations to the Guanacaste Dry Forest Conservation Fund help to save Costa Rica's biodiversity; tax-deductible donations can be matched from conservation foundations and will be used 100 percent for land acquisition (no overhead or administrative charges). Contact Dr. Daniel H. Janzen for further details; djan zen@sas.upenn.edu. Donations made out to the Guanacaste Dry Forest Conservation Fund can be sent to Prof. Daniel H. Janzen, Dept. of Biology, 415 South University Ave., University of Pennsylvania, Philadelphia, PA 19104. http://janzen.sas.upenn.edu/RR/rincon_rainforest.htm.

Tirimbina Rainforest Center: A tropical science research and tourism center initiated by the Milwaukee Public Museum. Telephone: 506-2761-1579 or 506-2761-0055; e-mail: info@tirimbina.org. www.envirolink.org.

APPENDIX B: WILDLIFE TOURISM SITES AND FIELD STATIONS OF COSTA RICA

The wildlife tourism sites described here and portrayed in the map include 76 sites that have been visited by the author in Costa Rica, many of which are referred to in this book. In the following key, the site code from Figure 11 is followed by the name of the site, its biological zone and elevation, its coordinates, a brief description, and contact information. Abbreviations: BR, Biological Reserve. NP, National Park. NWR, National Wildlife Refuge. OTS, Organization for Tropical Studies. PAH, Pan American Highway.

Figure 11. Wildlife tourism sites referred to in the text and on species distribution maps. Prefixes to site numbers refer to the five biological zones outlined on the map: G, Guanacaste; S, Southern Pacific lowlands; H, Highlands; P, Central Plateau; and C, Caribbean lowlands.

GUANACASTE REGION

G-1: Los Inocentes Ranch: Tropical moist forest. Elev. 750'. Lat. 11°02.50'N, long. 85°30.00'W. Address: P.O. Box 228-3000, Heredia, Costa Rica. This lodge is now closed to tourism.

G-2: Santa Rosa NP: Tropical dry forest/premontane moist forest. Elev. 1350'. Lat. 10°51.50'N, long. 85°36.50'W. This park contains 181,186 acres and is an excellent example of tropical dry forest and premontane moist forest, as well as gallery forests. The Olive Ridley Turtle nesting beaches of Nancite are within this park. Telephone: Santa Rosa NP, 506-2666-5051; Guanacaste Conservation Area, 506-2666-4740.

G-3: Liberia, road to Tamarindo: Tropical dry forest. Elev. 100'. From lat. 10°37.50'N, long. 85°27.00'W, to lat. 10°18.60'N, long. 85°55.00'W. Many species of the tropical dry forest can be spotted along this road en route to see the Leatherback Turtles at Tamarindo.

G-4: Tamarindo, Playa Grande, Las Baulas NP, and Sugar Beach: Tropical dry forest. Elev. Sea level. Lat. 10°18.60'N, long. 85°55.00'W. Las Baulas NP, which covers 1,364 acres, protects the nesting beaches of the Leatherback Turtle at Playa Grande. Mangrove lagoons and beaches in the vicinity are important wintering sites for shorebirds, wading birds, and local wildlife. Tropical dry forests of the area provide opportunities for viewing howler monkeys and other upland wildlife. Tamarindo NWR and Las Baulas National Marine Park, telephone: 506-2653-0470. Turtle tours available October through March at El Mundo de las Tortugas, 506-2653-0471, at Playa Grande. Hotel Bula Bula, 506-2653-0975, www.hotelbulabula.com; Hotel Las Tortugas, 506-2653-0423; Hotel Villa Baula, 506-2653-0644; www.hotelvillabaula.com.

G-5: Lomas Barbudal BR: Tropical dry forest. Elev. 100'. Lat. 10°26.20'N, long. 85°16.00'W. Lomas Barbudal is a reserve of 5,631 acres that provides an excellent example of riparian forest within the Guanacaste region. Elegant Trogons, Scrub Euphonias, and Long-tailed Manakins are among the featured wildlife there.

G-6: Palo Verde NP. Tropical dry forest. Elev. 30'. Lat. 10°22.21'N, long. 85°11.84'W. Palo Verde NP is one of the best examples of both dry forest and tropical wetlands. This park includes the area that was formerly designated as the Dr. Rafael Lucas Rodríguez Caballero NWR, with 45,511 acres of tropical dry forest, riparian forest, and marshes. It is an important wintering site for migratory waterfowl and local Black-bellied Whistling-Ducks and Muscovy Ducks; also home to Jabiru storks, Scarlet Macaws, and Snail Kites. This is an important research and education site for the OTS and for the National Biodiversity Institute. Palo Verde OTS Biological Station, telephone: 506-2524-0607; www.threepaths.co.cr. Reservations: edu.travel@ots.ac.cr.

G-7: La Pacífica (Hotel Hacienda La Pacífica) **and Cañas:**

Tropical dry forest. Elev. 150'. Lat. 10°27.21'N, long. 85°07.68'W. This lodge, on a 6,548-acre ranch and private forest reserve formerly known as Finca La Pacífica, is an excellent place to stay when visiting locations like Guanacaste, Santa Rosa, and Palo Verde NPs and Lomas Barbudal BR. Address: Apdo 8, 5700 Cañas, Guanacaste, Costa Rica; www.pacificacr.com. Telephone: 506-2669-6050; e-mail: pacifica@racsa.com.cr. On the east boundary of this property is Las Pumas, a wild cat rescue and rehabilitation center. All six of Costa Rica's wild cats can be observed there. Telephone: 506-2669-6044. Donations are appreciated.

G-8: Estancia Jiménez Nuñez and lagoons: Tropical dry forest. Elev. 250'. Lat. 10°20.55'N, long. 85°08.69'W. Private ranch with large man-made lagoons with many waterbirds; good raptor viewing on the road from the PAH west to this ranch. Get permission from the guard at the entrance to see the lagoons.

G-9: Hacienda Solimar: Tropical dry forest. Elev. 100'. Lat. 10°15.58'N, long. 85°09.40'W. Excellent dry forest and riparian forest, with exceptional wetland wildlife, including Roseate Spoonbills, Snail Kites, nesting Jabiru storks, Boat-billed Herons, Bare-throated Tiger-Herons, and crocodiles. Owners have made significant improvements to this 5,000-acre ranch to accommodate wildlife tourism. Telephone, at ranch: 506-2669-0281; e-mail: solimar@racsa.co.cr.

G-10: Río Lagarto bridge and farm lagoon: Premontane moist forest. Elev. 140'. Lat. 10°09.76'N, long. 84°54.93'W. This is a farm pond just off the PAH north of the bridge over the Río Lagarto. It is at Ganadería Avancari. Black-bellied Whistling-Ducks, Least Grebes, Purple Gallinules, and Northern

Jacanas are regularly observed along the road in the marsh.

G-11: Pulperia La Pita and lowlands to Monteverde: Tropical moist forest. Elev. 700'. From lat. 10°10.09'N, long. 84°54.38'W to lat. 10°18.00'N, long. 84°49.20'W. This is the road from the turnoff from the PAH by Río Lagarto, past a small store known as Pulperia La Pita and through mixed pasture and woodland en route to Monteverde. Wildlife includes species of the Guanacaste dry forest, like White-throated Magpie-Jays, Crested Bobwhites, Rufous-naped Wrens, and Long-tailed Manakins.

G-12: Puntarenas, Hotel Tioga, and Playa Doña Ana: Premontane wet forest. Elev. Sea level. Lat. 9°58.46'N, long. 84°50.34'W. The lagoons and beaches of Puntarenas and nearby Playa Doña Ana provide excellent areas to observe shorebirds, wading birds, White-winged Doves, frigatebirds, cormorants, Black Skimmers, Anhingas, terns, and gulls. Hotel Tioga, with its downtown beachfront location, provides easy access to the beach, local wetlands, and nearby birding sites like Carara NP. Address: P.O. Box 96-5400, Puntarenas, Costa Rica; www.hoteltioga.com. Telephone: in San José, 506-2255-3115; in Puntarenas, 506-2661-0271.

G-13: Bajamar: Tropical dry forest. Elev. Sea level. Lat. 9°50.50'N, long. 84°40.50'W. This area of tropical dry forest and mangrove lagoons near the coast represents the southern range limit for dry forest wildlife of the Guanacaste region.

G-14: La Ensenada Lodge: Tropical dry forest. Elev. Sea level to 250'. Lat. 10°08.304'N, long. 85°02.394'W. A privately owned national wildlife reserve, this 939-acre ranch is a wildlife mecca at the head of the Gulf of Nicoya. It contains tropical dry forest, pastures, mangrove lagoons, shoreline habitat, wetlands, and commercial salt ponds that attract great varieties of shorebirds. This ranch is used by Three-wattled Bellbirds from roughly December through February, as well as Turquoise-browed Motmots and White-throated Magpie-Jays. Boat tours in nearby mangrove lagoons provide the chance to see the Mangrove Vireo, Mangrove Hummingbird, Mangrove Cuckoo, and Mangrove race of the Yellow Warbler. This is one of the only places in Costa Rica where the Northern Potoo can be encountered at night. www .laensenada.net. Telephone: 506-2289-6655 or 506-2289-7443; e-mail: la_ensenada@yahoo.com.

G-15: Hotel Borinquen Mountain Resort and Thermal Spa: Tropical moist forest/premontane moist forest transition. Elev. 2,500'. Lat. 10°48.704'N, long. 84°04.965'W. This resort and spa features thermal springs and also provides good birding opportunities on the grounds and vicinity, including access to nearby Rincón de la Vieja NP. Wildlife is typical of the tropical dry forest but also features some species of the Caribbean slope. There are Turquoise-browed Motmots, Crested Caracaras, Red-lored Parrots, White-fronted Parrots, Keel-billed Toucans, White-throated Magpie-Jays, Double-striped Thick-knees, and Plain-capped Starthroats. www.borinquenresort.com. Telephone: 506-2690-1900; e-mail: borinque@racsa.co.cr.

SOUTHERN PACIFIC LOWLANDS

S-1: Carara NP, Río Tárcoles estuary, Tárcol Lodge, Villa Caletas, Crocodile Jungle Safari, and Villa Lapas: Carara NP: Premontane

moist forest. Elev. Sea level–100'. Lat. 9°47.72'N, long. 84°36.16'W. Carara NP is an excellent reserve, covering 12,953 acres, that has wildlife of both the Guanacaste tropical dry forest and tropical wet forests of the southern Pacific lowlands. It is one of the best places to observe Scarlet Macaws and crocodiles in the country. Telephone: Carara NP, 506-2383-9953; Villa Caletas is an excellent seaside resort that provides easy access to Carara NP and boat tours in the Río Tárcoles mangrove lagoons. Many notable wildlife species can be seen right on the grounds, including Zone-tailed Hawks, parrots, chachalacas, and hummingbirds. Address: P.O. Box 12358-1000, San José, Costa Rica; www.villacaletas .com. Telephone: Reservations, 506-2637-0606; Hotel, 506-2637-0505; e-mail: reservations@villa caletas.com. Crocodile Jungle Safari Tour: Tropical dry forest. Elev. Sea level. Lat. 9°46.930'N, long. 84°38.187'W. Crocodile Jungle Safari offers outstanding boat tours in the mangrove lagoons and estuaries of the Río Tárcoles near Carara NP. The guides are exceptional at bird identification and are successful in locating a variety of birds and providing great photo opportunities. This tour company provides good opportunities for viewing the crocodiles. They are recommended because they do not feed or habituate the crocodiles to their presence like some tour operators. Address: P.O. Box 1542, San Pedro, Costa Rica; www.costa ricanaturetour.com. Telephone: 506-2637-0338; e-mail: crocodile @costaricanaturetour.com. Hotel Villa Lapas: Tropical moist forest. Elev. approx. 150'. Lat. 9°45.368'N, long. 84°36.573'W. The grounds of this resort offer some outstanding birding and easy access to nearby

Carara NP and the Río Tárcoles mangrove lagoons. Trogons, owls, tiger-herons, and even Scarlet Macaws can be observed on the property. The skywalk facility in the adjacent forest provides outstanding opportunities to see wildlife of the moist and dry forest, including Long-tailed Manakins, hummingbirds, parrots, tanagers, and trogons. Address: P.O. Box 419-4005, Heredia, Costa Rica; www.villa lapas.com. Telephone: 506-2637-0232; e-mail:info@villalapas .com. Hotel Xandari by the Beach: South of Carara; www .hotelxandari.com. Telephone: 506-2778-7070.

S-2: Orotina, road to lowlands approaching Carara: Tropical moist forest. Elev. 500'. Lat. 9°51.80'N, long. 84°34.00'W. This route includes the famous city park in Orotina where a pair of Black-and-white Owls and an introduced Two-toed Sloth have lived for many years.

S-3: Parrita, road to Puriscal: Tropical moist forest. Site 1: Elev. 1,600'. Lat. 9°42.46'N, long. 84°24.22 W. Site 2: Elev. 2,000'. Lat. 9°43.90'N, long. 84.23.64'W.

S-4: Manuel Antonio NP, Rancho Casa Grande, Damas Island mangrove tours, and Quepos: Tropical wet forest. Elev. Sea level. Lat. 9°22.94'N, long. 84°08.62'W. Manuel Antonio NP covers 4,015 acres of land and 135,905 acres of ocean. It provides excellent opportunities to see squirrel monkeys, agoutis, white-faced monkeys, ctenosaurs, butterflies, and many species of the southern Pacific lowlands. Telephone: 506-2777-3130, 506-2777-1646; toll-free reservations, 1-888-790-5264; e-mail:osrap@ minae.go.cr. Foresta Resort Rancho Casa Grande: Premontane wet forest. Elev. approx. 100–250'. Lat. 9°26.414'N, long. 84°08.185'W. Hotel Rancho Casa

Grande is an excellent lodge to stay at while exploring the Quepos area, including Manuel Antonio NP and the nearby mangrove lagoons. There are some outstanding trails for birding on the 180 acres. It is a good place to see endangered squirrel monkeys, tityras, Streaked Flycatchers, and other wildlife of the southern Pacific lowlands. Address: P.O. Box 618-2010 Zapote, San José, Costa Rica; www.ranchocasa grande.com. Telephone: 506-2777-3130, 506-2777-1646; e-mail: hotelrcg@sol.racsa.co.cr. Damas Island mangrove lagoons: Iguana Tours (Jorge's Mangrove Tours) in Quepos can arrange boating tours to see the wildlife of the mangrove lagoons near Damas Island. It is one of the best places to look for the rare Silky Anteater, Mangrove Hummingbird, Mangrove Vireo, and the Mangrove subspecies of the Yellow Warbler. www.iguanatours.com. Telephone: 506-2777-1262; e-mail: iguana@racsa.co.cr.

S-5: Talari Mountain Lodge near San Isidro del General: Premontane wet forest. Elev. 2,800'. Lat. 9°24.14'N, long. 83°40.12'W. This rustic lodge near San Isidro has great wildlife viewing opportunities on the grounds. It is easy to observe seventy species in a morning of birding there. This is an excellent place to see the Slaty Spinetail, Pearl Kite, and Red-legged Honeycreeper. Many birds come to the feeders. Address: Talari Albergue de Montaña, Rivas, San Isidro del General, Apdo 517-8000, Pérez Zeledón, Costa Rica; www.talari.co.cr. Telephone and fax: 506-2771-0341; e-mail: talaricostarica@gmail.com. This is a good place to stay if visiting Los Cusingos, the former home of famous ornithologist Alexander Skutch, now managed by the Tropical Science

Center in San José (see details for site S-7).

S-6: La Junta de Pacuares resort on Río General: Tropical moist forest. Elev. 2,200'. Lat. 9°16.51'N, long. 83°38.33'W. A variety of wildlife can be seen along the river at this site, including Gray-headed Chachalacas.

S-7: Los Cusingos, San Isidro del General, City Lagoons, and Hotel del Sur: Tropical moist forest. San Isidro del General: Elev. 2,200'. Lat. 9°20.40'N, long. 83°28.00'W.; City sewage lagoons: Elev. 2,000'. Lat. 9°22.25'N, long. 83°41.80'W.; Los Cusingos: Elev. 2,500'. Lat. 9°19.10'N, long. 83°36.75'W. Los Cusingos Neotropical Bird Sanctuary is the former homestead of the late Dr. Alexander and Pamela Skutch. It is now managed by the Tropical Science Center. Los Cusingos is an excellent remnant forest reserve where it is possible to make a day trip to see Bay-headed Tanagers, Gray-headed Chachalacas, Speckled Tanagers, White-breasted Wood-Wrens, and other wildlife of the southern Pacific moist forest. Make arrangements for visits with the Tropical Science Center, Apdo 8-3870-1000, San José, Costa Rica; www.cct.or.cr (Refugio Los Cusingos). Telephone: 506-2253-3267; e-mail: cct@cct.oor.cr. Hotel del Sur in San Isidro del General and Talari Mountain Lodge (site S-5) provide convenient places to stay. Address: Hotel del Sur, P.O. Box 4-8000, San Isidro del General, Costa Rica; Google "Hotel del Sur, Costa Rica." Telephone: 506-2771-3033; e-mail: reservas@hoteldel-sur.com.

S-8: Río Térraba bridge crossing: Tropical moist forest. Elev. 200'. Bridge over Río Térraba: Lat. 9°00.20'N, long. 83°13.20'W. This bridge crossing is well known for the huge crocodiles that can be

seen there, as well as herons and egrets.

S-9: Wilson Botanical Garden at San Vito–OTS Las Cruces Biological Field Station: Premontane rainforest. Elev. 3,900'. Wilson Botanical Garden, lat. 8°49.61'N, long. 82°57.80'W. This OTS field station has cabins for tourists and an excellent trail system. There are regionally endemic birds on the property, and many birds come to the feeders there. Address: Apdo 73-8257, San Vito, Costa Rica; main OTS address: Apdo 676-2050 San Pedro de Montes Oca, Costa Rica; www.three paths.com. Telephone: in USA, 1-919-684-5774; in San José, 506-2524-0607; reservations in San José, 506-2524-0628; e-mail: edu .travel@ots.ac.cr. Wetland birds can be observed nearby at the lagoons by the airport (for a fee; this is on private property) and at Los Contaros, a private nature park and wetland with a gift shop owned by Gail Hewson. It has indigenous crafts of the Guaymi community and is on the outskirts of San Vito, near the Wilson Botanical Garden.

S-10: Sabalito, road from San Vito: Premontane wet forest. Elev. 2,200'. From lat. 8°49.61'N, long. 82°57.80'W, to lat. 8°49.80'N, long. 82°53.80'W. When exploring the San Vito area, along this road is a good place to look for southern specialties like the Bran-colored Flycatcher, Pearl Kite, Masked (Chiriquí) Yellowthroat, and Crested Oropendola.

S-11: Paso Canoas: Premontane wet forest. Elev. 300'. From lat. 8°32.00'N, long. 82°50.30'W, to lat. 8°49.61'N, long. 82°57.80'W. Paso Canoas is the town in southern Costa Rica where the PAH enters Panama. Wildlife of the area is typical of the southern Pacific lowlands.

S-12: Sierpe, on the Río Térraba, to Drake Bay: Premontane wet forest. Elev. Sea level. From Sierpe at lat. 8°51.50'N, long. 83°28.20'W, to the Río Sierpe estuary at lat. 8°46.50'N, long. 83°38.00'W. Local lodging includes Río Sierpe Lodge, where boat trips are available to Corcovado NP and Caño Island Biological Reserve. Telephone: 506-2283-5573; e-mail: vsftrip@racsa.co.cr.

S-13: Drake Bay Wilderness Resort, northwest end of Corcovado NP: Tropical wet forest. Elev. Sea level. Lat. 8°41.80'N, long. 83°41.00'W. www.drakebay.com. Telephone: 506-2770-8012 (also fax), 506-2384-4107; in San José, 506-2256-7394; at resort, 506-2371-3437; e-mail: hdrake@sol.racsa.co.cr.

S-14: Caño Island Biological Reserve: Tropical wet forest. Elev. Sea level. Lat. 8°43.000'N, long. 83°53.000'W. This island includes 741 acres and is six miles from the Osa Peninsula. It is possible to see hump-backed whales while en route between the mainland and the island. Arrange for visits with local lodges like Río Sierpe Lodge, Drake Bay Wilderness Resort, Aguila de Osa Inn, La Paloma Lodge, or Marenco Lodge.

S-15: Sirena Biological Station, Corcovado NP: Tropical wet forest. Elev. Sea level. Lat. 8°78.740'N, long. 35.810'W. This biological station is one of the best examples of remote, wild rainforest in Costa Rica. There are significant populations of Scarlet Macaws, tapirs, White-lipped Peccaries, Great Curassows, Jaguars, Cougars, and other species characteristic of tropical wet forests. Accessible by air or on foot by hiking along the beach from La Leona or San Pedrillo.

S-16: Corcovado Lodge Tent Camp, Carate, and southeast end of Corcovado NP: Tropical wet forest. Elev. Sea level. Lat. 8°26.880'N, long. 83°28.970'W. This excellent tent camp lodge provides great access for wildlife viewing on the beachfront property, along trails in the rainforest behind the lodge, and in nearby Corcovado NP. A wildlife tower allows viewing of wildlife in the forest canopy. Wildlife includes Scarlet Macaws, parrots, King Vultures, and many raptors. Address: Costa Rica Expeditions, P.O. Box 6941-1000, San José, Costa Rica; www.costaricaexpeditions.com. Telephone: 506-2257-0766, 506-2222-0333; e-mail: costaric@expeditions.co.cr. Similar wildlife can be observed at Marenco Beach and Rainforest Lodge (506-2770-8002; www.marencolodge.com), Bosque del Cabo (506-2735-5206; www.bosquedelcabo.com), Luna Lodge (506-2380-5036; www.lunalodge.com), La Paloma Lodge (506-2239-2801; www.lapalomalodge.com), and Lapa Ríos (506-2735-513; www.laparios.com).

S-17: Tiskita Jungle Lodge: Tropical wet forest. Elev. Sea level to 200'. Lat. 8°21.480'N, long. 83°8.050'W. A 400-acre private forest reserve and tropical fruit experimental field station, this is one of the best places in Costa Rica to see squirrel monkeys and White Hawks. Many tanagers and honeycreepers are present because of the variety of fruiting trees on the grounds. Address: Costa Rica Sun Tours, P.O. Box 13411-1000, San José, Costa Rica; www.tiskita.com. Telephone: 506-2296-8125.

S-18: Road from San Vito to Paso Canoas: Premontane moist forest. Elev. 900'. Lat. 8°44.500'N, long. 82°56.900'W. The highway from San Vito de Java to Paso Canoas provides a good opportunity for viewing wildlife of the southern Pacific lowlands, including Blue-headed Parrots, squirrel monkeys, and relatively new arrivals in Costa Rica like the Pearl Kite and Crested Oropendola. There is a colony of Crested Oropendolas nesting along the highway near Villa Neily.

S-19: Esquinas Rainforest Lodge: Tropical wet forest. Elev. 800'. Lat. 9°33.131'N, long. 83°48.624'W. This is an excellent ecolodge at the head of the Osa Peninsula near the town of Gamba and Piedras Blancas NP. It has a great variety of wildlife of the southern Pacific lowlands, ranging from Spectacled Owls to antbirds, hummingbirds, Baird's Trogons, and the endemic Black-cheeked Ant-Tanager. www.esquinaslodge.com. Telephone: 506-2741-8001.

S-20: La Cusinga, Oro Verde, Cristal Ballena, Ballena Marine NP: La Cusinga Lodge: Tropical wet forest. Elev. Sea level–400'. Lat. 9°8.500'N, long. 83°42.900'W. This outstanding ecolodge, an ecologically sustainable facility that is sensitive to environmental protection, provides a rustic and attractive setting overlooking the Pacific Ocean. It is possible to see a great variety of rainforest wildlife, including Great Tinamous, Spectacled Owls, manakins, toucans, and oropendolas in the vicinity of the cabins, along the beach, and along the trails. The owners of this property, John Tressemer and his son, Geiner Guzman, were instrumental in the establishment of the Ballena Marine NP. Address: La Cusinga, S.A., Apdo 41-8000, San Isidro del General, Costa Rica; www.lacusingalodge.com. Telephone: 506-2770-2549. While staying at La Cusinga, it is possible to take a whale- and dolphin-watching excursion to see the migrant humpback whales, false killer whales, dolphins, and marine birds of the offshore areas in Ballena Marine NP. This national park was created in 1991 by President Oscar Arias after photos taken by the author on a Henderson Birding Tour in 1990 documented the winter calving grounds of humpback whales offshore from Caño Island and Punta Uvita. The park includes 425 acres of oceanfront land and 12,750 acres of ocean. For a boat tour to see the whales and dolphins, contact Delfín Tours (506-2743-8169), Ballena Tour (506-2831-1617), or Pelican Tours (506-2743-8047; cabinaslarr@hotmail.com). Other resorts in this vicinity include Cristal Ballena Hotel Resort: Lat. 9°7.441'N, long. 83°41.855'W. www.cristal-ballena.com. Telephone: 506-2786-5354. Whales and Dolphins: A four-star hotel. www.whalesand dolphins.net. Telephone: in USA (toll-free), 1-866-429-3958; in Costa Rica, 506-2743-8150; e-mail: sales@whalesanddol phins.net. Oro Verde Tropical Rainforest Reserve: Tropical wet forest. Lat. 9°12.400'N, long. 83°45.600'W. Elev. 1,000'–2,200'. This private rainforest reserve is about two miles northwest of the village of Uvita along the coast road and two miles east. It does not have lodging available but is a good destination for a day trip to explore the rainforest. It has good trails and an observation tower. Distinctive birds of this site are the Black-crested Coquette, Blue-throated Goldentail, Brown-hooded Parrot, Chestnut-mandibled Toucan, Blue-crowned Motmot, and Crested Owl. www .costarica-birding-oroverde.com. Telephone: 506-2743-8072, 506-2843-8833, 506-2827-3325.

S-21: Hacienda Barú NWR: Tropical wet forest. Elev. Sea level. Lat. 9°15.984'N, long. 83°53.028'W. Playa Dominical and Hacienda Barú NWR are beach areas with migrant shorebirds, like Willets and Whimbrels, and adjacent forest with abundant birdlife. Hacienda Barú Resort; www .haciendabaru.com. Telephone: 506-2787-0003.

S-22: Playa Hermosa: Tropical wet forest. Elev. Sea level. Lat. 9°34.495'N, 84°36.673'W. Playa Hermosa and adjacent pastures are noted for wetland birds, many wintering Barn Swallows, and recent records of Southern Lapwings.

CENTRAL PLATEAU

P-1: Sarchí vicinity: Premontane wet forest. Elev. 3,100'. Lat. 10°5.10'N, long. 84°20.80'W. Birds of this urban area include the Blue-gray Tanager, Summer Tanager, Baltimore Oriole, Grayish Saltator, Rufous-tailed Hummingbird, Yellow Warbler, and Clay-colored Thrush.

P-2: Xandari Plantation Resort, Juan Santamaría International Airport–Pavas vicinity, Hotel Alta, and Tobías Bolaños Airport: Premontane moist forest. Elev. 3,200'. Lat. 9°59.60'N, long. 84°08.40'W. The Xandari Plantation Resort has beautifully landscaped grounds with many ornamental flowers and birds. Blue-crowned Motmots, Ferruginous Pygmy-Owls, Tropical Screech-Owls, and even Long-tailed Manakins can be encountered there. The shade coffee plantation on the grounds is one of the only places in Costa Rica to find the Buffy-crowned Wood-Partridge. Address: Xandari Plantation, Apdo 1485-4050, Alajuela, Costa Rica; www.xan dari.com. Telephone: 506-2443-2020; e-mail: hotel@xandari .com. Telephone: 506-2443-2020. Hotel Alta has beautifully landscaped grounds and is an excellent hotel near the airport. www.thealtahotel.com. Telephone: 506-2282-4160; e-mail: info@thealtahotel.com. Hotel Aeropuerto: www.hotelaeropuer to-cr.com; telephone: 2433-7333.

P-3: San José vicinity and downtown: Premontane moist forest (urban). Elev. 3,700'. Lat. 9°56.96'N, longitude 84°04.05'W.

P-4: Tres Ríos, Curridibat: Premontane moist forest. Elev. 3,900'. Lat. 9°54.14'N, long. 84°00.37'W.

P-5: Cartago vicinity, Lankester Gardens, and Las Concavas marsh: Premontane moist forest. Elev. 4,700'. Lat. 9°50.20'N, long. 83°53.55'W. The Parque de Expression in Cartago has ponds with waterbirds like Northern Jacanas. The private Las Concavas marsh and adjacent pastures can be viewed with permission; look for wintering Blue-winged Teal, Killdeer, Eastern Meadowlarks, and Least Grebes.

P-6: Hotel Bougainvillea: Premontane moist forest. Elev. 3,910'. Lat. 9°58.244'N, long. 84°04.965'W. Hotel Bougainvillea in Santo Domingo de Heredia is an excellent hotel for beginning or ending a stay in Costa Rica. The eight acres of gardens are beautifully landscaped and attract a great variety of birds, including Blue-crowned Motmots, Grayish Saltators, Ferruginous Pygmy-Owls, and rare White-eared and Prevost's Ground-Sparrows, which regularly visit the compost pile on the east side of the garden. Mailing address: P.O. Box 69-2120, San José, Costa Rica; www.hb.co.cr. Telephone: in USA (toll-free), 1-866-880-5441; in Costa Rica, 506-2244-1414; e-mail: info@hb.co.cr. Motel staff can arrange for rides to the nearby INBIO Parque, the biodiversity park and interpretive center of the National Biodiversity Institute in Santo Domingo de Heredia. www.inbio.ac.cr; www.inbioparque.com; Telephone: INBIO, 506-2507-8100 or 506-2507-8107; INBIO Parque, 506-2507-8107.

CARIBBEAN LOWLANDS

C-1: Inocentes–Río Frío region; road from Los Inocentes Ranch east to lowlands by Santa Cecilia: Tropical moist forest. From lat. 11°02.70'N, long. 85°30.00'W. at Los Inocentes Ranch (now closed to tourism) to lat. 11°03.70'N, long. 85°24.40'W. at Santa Cecilia. This region has wildlife species of the Caribbean lowlands. Owls and Common and Great Potoos can be seen along the road at night with the aid of spotlights.

C-2: Caño Negro NWR and Natural Lodge Caño Negro: Tropical moist forest. Elev. 175'. Lat. 10°54.50'N, long. 84°47.70'W. An exceptional refuge of 24,483 acres, providing habitat for wetland wildlife of the Caribbean lowlands, including waterfowl, wading birds, and rare species like the Nicaraguan Seed-Finch, Nicaraguan Grackle, Agami Heron, and Green Ibis. There is a recent record of nesting by Jabiru storks. The Caño Negro wetlands have been designated one of the most important wetlands in the world. Lodging, boat trips, and tarpon fishing in the nearby lake and channels of the Río Frío can be arranged at Natural Lodge Caño Negro; www.canonegrolodge.com. Telephone: central office, 506-2265-1204, 506-2265-3302, 506-2265-1298; hotel, 506-2471-1000, 506-2471-1426; e-mail: info@canonegrolodge.com.

C-3: Laguna del Lagarto and Ara Ambigua Lodges: Tropical wet forest. Elev. 200'. Lat. 10°41.20'N,

long. 84°11.20'W. The area of La Laguna del Lagarto Lodge has wildlife species of the Caribbean lowland rainforest and many wetland species. Address: P.O. Box 995-1007 Centro Colón, San José, Costa Rica; www.lagarto-lodge-costa-rica.com. Telephone: 506-2289-8163; e-mail: info@lagarto-lodge-costa-rica.com. Ara Ambigua, a rainforest lodge, is north of Puerto Viejo de Sarapiquí; it has a frog garden and opportunities for viewing wildlife along the Río Sarapiquí and forest trails. www.hotelaraambigua.com. Telephone: 506-2766-7101, 506-2766-6401; e-mail: info@hotelaraambigua.com.

C-4: Tortuga Lodge and Tortuguero NP: Tropical wet forest. Elev. Sea level. Lat. 10°34.36'N, long. 83°31.04'W. An exceptional area of lowland wet forest with great opportunities to view macaws, monkeys, toucans, bats, crocodiles, hummingbirds, and butterflies along the canals and foot trails behind Tortuga Lodge. Address: Costa Rica Expeditions, Apdo 6941-1000, San José, Costa Rica, or Dept. 235, Box 025216, Miami, FL 33102-5216; www.costaricaexpeditions.com. Telephone: 506-2222-0333, 506-2257-0766; e-mail: costaric@expeditions.co.cr.

C-5: La Selva, Selva Verde, Sueño Azul, Puerto Viejo, and Rancho Gavilán: Tropical wet forest. Elev. 200'. Lat. 10°25.89'N, long. 84°00.27'W. La Selva Biological Field Station is a biological research station operated by OTS. The author first studied tropical ecology in a course at La Selva in 1969. It is a great destination for observing wildlife of the Caribbean lowlands along well-maintained trails and boardwalks through the forest. There is an excellent opportunity to see owls, motmots, hummingbirds, trogons,

antbirds, tinamous, collared peccaries, and other rainforest species. Address: Organization for Tropical Studies, Apdo 676-2050, San Pedro de Montes de Oca, San José, Costa Rica; www.threepaths.co.cr. Telephone: in USA, 1-919-684-5774; in Costa Rica, 506-2524-0607; e-mail: edu.travel@ots.ac.cr. Selva Verde Lodge, Sueño Azul Resort, and El Gavilán Lodge are all excellent places to stay while visiting La Selva. It is also possible to stay in cabins at the La Selva OTS facility by contacting the OTS for reservations. Selva Verde Lodge address: Chilamate, Sarapiquí, Costa Rica; www.selvaverde.com. Telephone: in USA (toll-free), 1-800-2451-7111; in Costa Rica, 506-2766-6800; e-mail: selvaver@racsa.co.cr. El Gavilán Lodge, www.gavilanlodge.com. Telephone: 506-2766-6743, 506-2234-9507; e-mail: gavilan@racsa.co.cr. Sueño Azul Resort is an outstanding lodge a few miles south of La Selva. The grounds and adjacent pastures and river provide excellent birding for such specialties as Fasciated Tiger-Herons, trogons, motmots, guans, Scaled Pigeons, Black-faced Grosbeaks, and Sunbitterns. www.suenoazulresort.com. Telephone: in San José, 506-2253-2020; hotel, 506-2764-1000, 506-2764-1048, 506-2764-1049; e-mail: info@suenoazulresort.com.

C-6: Guacimo, road from La Selva to Guacimo lowland turnoff: Tropical wet forest. Elev. 200'. From lat. 10°25.89'N, long. 84°00.27'W, to lat. 10°13.00'N, long. 83°56.00'W. This is an area of cleared pastureland and scrub, small ponds, and some rivers—good for herons, egrets, anis, and an occasional King Vulture. La Tirimbina Biological Reserve; www.tirimbina.org. Telephone: 506-2761-1579; e-mail: info@tirimbina.org.

C-7: Rara Avis: Premontane rainforest. Elev. 2,000'. Lat. 10°17.30'N, long. 84°02.47'W. This 1,500-acre reserve is an excellent place to observe wildlife of the Caribbean lowlands and foot-hills, including the rare Snowcap Hummingbird. Address: Apdo 8105-1000, San José, Costa Rica; www.rara-avis.com. Telephone: 506-2764-1111; e-mail: info@rara-avis.com.

C-8: Rainforest Aerial Tram, Tapir Trail, and Braulio Carrillo NP: Tropical wet forest. Elev. 2,000'. Lat. 10°10.80'N, long. 83°56.60'W. The tram and trails on the property provide excellent places to observe wildlife of middle elevations. Address: Apdo Postal 1959-1002, San José, Costa Rica; www.rfat.com. Telephone: 506-2257-5961; e-mail: info@rfat.com. At Tapir Trail, a private reserve along the highway east of Braulio Carrillo NP, it is possible to see Black-crested Coquettes and Snowcaps.

C-9: Guapiles and Guacimo lowlands: Tropical wet forest. Elev. 900'. Lat. 10°12.85'N, long. 83°47.35'W. The highway from Guapiles east to Limón is excellent for spotting sloths along the highway. Rare Fasciated Tiger-Herons can sometimes be seen on rocks near the Río Roca bridge. East of Guapiles is the famous EARTH University, a trop-ical sustainable research station for agriculture that also provides rooms for tourists and excellent birding opportunities on a forest reserve of more than 1,000 acres. www.earth.ac.cr. Telephone: 506-2713-0000.

C-10: Road from Limón to Cahuita: Tropical moist forest. Elev. Sea level. From lat. 9°59.20'N, long. 83°02.00'W, to lat. 9°45.00'N, long. 82°50.20'W. Along this coastal highway it is possible to see Collared Araçaris, Blue-

headed Parrots, and many shorebirds and wading birds in the estuaries that flow into the Caribbean. See safety warning for Cahuita, site C-11.

C-11: Cahuita NP, El Pizote Lodge: Tropical moist forest. Elev. Sea level. Lat. 9°45.00' long. 82°50.20'. This national park, encompassing 2,637 acres, was designated for protection of the coral reef there. It is the best example of coral reef in the country, but it has suffered in recent times from chemi-cal pollution and siltation from banana plantations. This is one of the best places in the country to observe sloths, and there are many shorebirds, tanagers, and other wildlife species that can be seen. In late October the Cahuita and Puerto Viejo area is a major passage site for raptors migrating from North America to Panama and South America. Over a mil-lion raptors were counted passing through this area during late October 2000 (Jennifer McNicoll-Giancarlo, personal communica-tion). Warning: Violence associ-ated with the local drug culture can make this area unsafe for careless tourists who visit local bars and stray from major hotels and public beaches. El Pizote Lodge is a good lodge there. www.pizotelodge.com. Telephone: 506-2750-0088; e-mail: pizotelg@hotmail.com. Another good lodging facility is Punta Cocles. www.hotelpunta-cocles.com. Telephone: 1-888-790-5264; reservations: booking@hotelpuntacocles.com.

C-12: Valle Escondido: Tropi-cal wet forest. Elev. 1,700'. Lat. 10°16.500'N, long. 84°31.800'W. Valle Escondido Lodge is a rain-forest resort at the town of San Lorenzo, north of San Ramón. It provides opportunities for bird-ing on 150 acres of primary rain-forest and adjacent mixed forest

pastures. Birds are characteristic of the Caribbean lowlands, including Keel-billed Toucans, Red-billed Pigeons, Red-lored Parrots, and White-crowned Par-rots. Address: Apdo 452, 1150 La Uruca, Costa Rica; www.costaricareisen.com (go to "hotels"). Telephone: 506-2231-0906.

C-13: Siquirres: Premontane wet forest. Elev. 500'. Lat. 10°6.000'N, 83°30.000'W. This site includes downtown Siquirres, where Tropical Mockingbirds can be seen in the church courtyard. In pasterelands to the northeast it is possible to see Red-breasted Blackbirds. The Costa Rican Amphibian Research Center, eight miles south of Siquirres, has the highest documented diversity of amphibians in Costa Rica. It is also regularly visited by flocks of Great Green Macaws. www.cramphibian.com.

C-14: Río Parismina: Tropical wet forest. Elev: Sea level. Lat. 10°18.388'N, long. 83°21.302'W. The canal from Tortuguero NP to Moin north of Limón provides an excellent opportunity for watching wildlife from a boat. The mouth of the Río Parismina is particularly rich in aquatic birdlife, including Black-necked Stilts, Greater Yellowlegs, Snowy Egrets, Tricolored Herons, Royal Terns, and Willets.

C-15: Jalova: Tropical wet forest. Elev: Sea level. Lat. 10°20.642'N, long. 83°23.935'W. The Jalova ("four corners") field office of Tortuguero NP is along the canal that leads from Tortuguero NP to Moin. Boating along the canal and in the courtyard at the office provides opportunities to see crocodiles, Blue-winged Teal, Golden-hooded Tanagers, Green Honeycreepers, Plumbeous Kites, American Pygmy King-fishers, and Mangrove Swallows. Even the rare manatee has been seen along the canal between this site and Tortuguero NP.

C-16: Río San Juan: Tropical wet forest. Elev: Sea level. Lat. 10°53.765'N, long. 83°40.826'W. This site is along the Río San Juan near its mouth at the Caribbean, in far northeastern Costa Rica. It is near Río Indio Lodge, which is north across the river in Nicaragua. Wildlife of the area includes the Common Black-Hawk, Mantled Howler Monkey, Collared Forest-Falcon, crocodile, three-toed sloth, Bare-throated Tiger-Heron, Purple-throated Fruitcrow, Strawberry Poison Dart Frogs, and the rare White-flanked Antwren. Río Indio Lodge, www.rioindiolodge. com. Telephone: in USA, 1-800-2593-3176; lodge, 506-2296-3338, 506-2296-0095; e-mail: info@ rioindiolodge.com.

C-17: Río Sarapiquí: Tropical wet forest. Elev: Sea level. Lat. 10°42.918'N, long. 83°56.314'W. This site is near the mouth of the Río Sarapiquí, where it enters the Río San Juan on the Nicaragua border. Wildlife that can be seen by boat include crocodiles, Green and Amazon Kingfishers, King Vultures, Green Iguanas, Brazilian Long-nosed Bats, and Mantled Howler Monkeys.

C-18: Tilajari Resort: Tropical moist forest. Elev: 350'. Lat. 10°28.308'N, long. 84°28.099'. The Hotel Tilajari Resort is an excellent resort that provides good access to the surrounding Arenal volcano area and to the Caño Negro NWR. The grounds provide good birding on forty acres along the Río San Carlos. The lodge also provides access for birding on a 600-acre cattle ranch and a 1,000-acre rainforest reserve. Address: Muelle, San Carlos, Costa Rica; www.tilajari .com. Telephone: 506-2462-1212; e-mail: info@tilajari.com.

C-19: Lost Iguana, Hanging Bridges, Arenal: Tropical wet forest. Elev. 1,600'. Lat. 10°29.128' long. 84°45.316'. Lost Iguana Resort is a delightful rainforest lodge that provides a spectacular view of the Arenal volcano and excellent birding on the 100 acres of habitat on the grounds. Early morning excursions by the lodge can offer sightings of Great Antshrikes, Barred Antshrikes, Dusky Antbirds, Purple-crowned Fairies, and Crested Guans. www.lostiguanaresort. com. Telephone: 506-2479-1555; e-mail: maritzalostiguana@mac. com. Volcano Arenal is the third most active volcano in the world and is part of the 30,000-acre Arenal Volcano NP. Lost Iguana Resort is close to the 250-acre Arenal Hanging Bridges rainforest. The trails and suspended bridges there provide access to great birding in a rainforest setting. www.hangingbridges. com. Telephone: 506-2479-9686. Another excellent lodge in the vicinity is the Arenal Observatory Lodge, owned and operated by one of Costa Rica's most prominent tourism companies, Costa Rica Sun Tours. Address: Apdo 13411-1000, San José, Costa Rica; www.arenalobservatory lodge.com. Telephone: 506-2692-2070, 506-2290-7011. Another birding location is B&B The Birdhouse. It features tropical gardens, bird feeders, orchids, and trails. Telephone: 506-2694-4428.

HIGHLANDS

H-1: Monteverde Cloud Forest Reserve: Lower montane rainforest. Elev. 4,500'. Lat. 10°19.00'N, long. 84°49.19'W. Monteverde Cloud Forest Reserve (Tropical Science Center) is an excellent example of cloud forest, with

Resplendent Quetzals, Three-wattled Bellbirds, Black Guans, and many hummingbirds, including the endemic Coppery-headed Emerald. Telephone: 506-2645-5122; e-mail: montever@sol .racsa.co.cr. Santa Elena Cloud Forest Reserve: www.montever deinfo.com; telephone: 506-2645-5390. There are many excellent hotels in the vicinity, including: Monteverde Lodge: address: Apdo 6941-1000, San José, Costa Rica; www.costaricaexpeditions. com; telephone: 506-2645-5057, 506-2257-0766; e-mail: costaric@ expeditions.co.cr. Humming-bird Gallery: www.fondavela. com; telephone: 506-2645-5030. Hotel Fonda Vela: address: Apdo 70060-1000, San José, Costa Rica; telephone: 506-2645-5125; e-mail: info@fondavela.com. Hotel Belmar: address: Apdo 17-5655, Monteverde, Costa Rica; www.centralamerica.com; telephone: 506-2645-5201; e-mail: belmar@racsa.co.cr.

H-2: Poás NP and Poás Volcano Lodge: Montane rainforest. Elev. 8,200'. Lat. 10°11.45'N, long. 84°13.95'W. Excellent example of montane forest, includes 16,076 acres. It is a good place to see Sooty Thrushes, Yellow-thighed Finches, Large-footed Finches, Magnificent and Volcano Hummingbirds, Slaty Flowerpiercers, and Bare-shanked Screech-Owls. An easy day trip while staying in San José. Poás Volcano Lodge: Lower montane wet forest. Elev. 6,342'. Lat. 10°09.746'N, long. 84°09.516'W. This facility provides convenient lodging near Vara Blanca while visiting Poás NP. Wildlife can be enjoyed in the excellent gardens on the grounds of the lodge, including Black Guans, Violet Sabrewings, Purple-throated Mountain-gems, Ruddy-capped Nightingale-Thrushes, and Bare-shanked Screech-Owls. Address: Apdo 1935-3000, Heredia, Costa Rica; www.poasvolcanolodge. com. Telephone: 506-2482-2194; e-mail: info@poasvolcanolodge .com.

H-3: La Virgen del Socorro: Premontane wet forest. Elev. 2,600', road descending to 2,200'. Lat. 10°15.68'N, long. 84°10.47'W. This road has long been a popular birding trail in the Caribbean foothills. Birds that can be seen in the forest along this road include the White Hawk, Violet-headed Hummingbird, and Black-crested Coquette. From the bridge at the lower end of the road it is possible to see Torrent Tyrannulets and dippers.

H-4: La Paz Waterfall Gardens, Vista Cinchona, and Peace Waterfall: Lower montane rainforest. Elev. 4,760'. Lat. 10°12.260'N, long. 84°9.695'W. This outstanding site on the east slope of Volcano Poás has 3.5 kilometers of trails and seventy acres of rainforest, with excellent trails for viewing wildlife of higher elevations, including rare species like the Sooty-faced Finch, dipper, and Azure-hooded Jay. At feeders it is possible to see Crimson-collared Tanagers and Prong-billed Barbets. A hummingbird feeder area hosts local specialties like the Green Thorntail, Brown Violet-ear, White-bellied Mountain-gem, Black-bellied Emerald, and endemic Coppery-headed Emerald. There is also a serpentarium, butterfly observatory, and large aviary. Restaurant and cabins are available. www.waterfallgardens. com. Telephone: 506-2482-2720, ext. 573; 506-2482-2721; e-mail: wgardens@racsa.co.cr. Peace Waterfall (Catarata de la Paz): Lower montane rainforest. Elev. 4,500'. Lat. 10°15.60'N, long. 84°10.70'W. This site can be good for viewing tanagers,

hummingbirds, Torrent Tyrannulets, and dippers.

H-5: El Portico Hotel, San José de la Montaña: Lower montane rainforest. Elev. 5,800'. Lat. 10°05.00'N, long. 84°07.00'W. An excellent location for higher elevation tanagers, hummingbirds, migrant warblers, and raptors.

H-6: La Ponderosa farm near Turrialba: Premontane wet forest. Elev. 3,760'. Lat. 9°57.31'N, long. 83°42.42'W.

Private land. Not accessible for tourism purposes.

H-7: Rancho Naturalista Mountain Lodge: Premontane wet forest. Elev. 3,200'. Lat. 9°49.92'N, long. 83°33.85'W. This is an exceptional site in the Caribbean foothills that has species of both lowlands and higher elevations. It is one of the best places in the country to see many hummingbirds, including the rare Snowcap. It is the only place where the rare Tawny-chested Flycatcher can be regularly seen. Many birds come to the feeders in the courtyard, and the viewing of hummingbirds at the hummingbird pools in the forest is unique in the country. Excellent naturalist guides and trails. Address: 3428 Hwy 465. Sheridan, AR 72150; www.costa ricagateway.com. Telephone: in the USA (toll-free), 1-888-246-8513; reservations, 506-2433-8278; e-mail: crgateway@racsa.co.cr.

H-8: Tapantí NP and Kiri Lodge: Premontane wet forest. Entrance elev. 4,300'. Lat. 9°45.620'N, long. 83°47.038'W. Bridge over the Río Grande de Orosí elev. 5,000'. Lat. 9°42.21' long. 83°46.93'. This national park covers 12,577 acres and is a great place to see wildlife of montane forests, like Collared Trogons, Costa Rican Pygmy-Owls, Red-headed and Prong-billed Barbets, Spangle-cheeked Tanagers, dippers, and Azure-hooded Jays. Kiri Lodge

telephone: 506-2533-2272. Google "Kiri Lodge, Costa Rica."

H-9: Cerro de la Muerte, San Gerardo de Dota region: Montane rainforest. Four popular birding sites, on the PAH. Kilometer 66 elev., road descending from 8,300' to 7,700'. Lat. 9°40.24'N, long. 83°51.92'W. This site, Finca El Jaular, is a private road on the west side of the PAH that is closed by a large gate. The road can be birded on foot—by permission only—by making arrangements to pay an entrance fee ahead of time (call Savegre Mountain Lodge at the telephone numbers listed for site H-10). Vehicles must be left at the main highway. The land is owned by the Vindas family, who live in the valley at the end of the road. The road descends through excellent primary montane rainforest and is a good place to see quetzals and other highland wildlife. Kilometer 76 elev., 9,400'. Lat. 9°35.68'N, long. 83°48.59'W. Near Los Chespiritos Restaurant 1 is a turnoff to Providencia. Along this road it is possible to see Silvery-throated Jays, Slaty Flowerpiercers, Yellow-thighed Finches, Fiery-throated Hummingbirds, and Black-billed Nightingale-Thrushes. The road is twelve kilometers long, but some of the best birding is in the first two kilometers from the PAH. Kilometer 86 elev. 9,100'. Lat. 9°36.88'N, long. 83°49.07'W. This site is a trail on the west side of the PAH, across the road and a couple hundred feet south of Los Chespiritos Restaurant 2. It is an excellent place to encounter the Timberline Wren, Peg-billed Finch, and high-elevation wildflowers. Kilometer 96 elev. 9,300'. Lat. 9°33.46'N, long. 83°42.67'W. This is west across the PAH from La Georgina restaurant and Villa Mills, at the site of an old highway construction camp where there is shrubby cover that is excellent for Volcano and Scintillant Hummingbirds and Timberline Wrens.

H-10: Savegre: Lower montane rainforest. Elev. 9,400'–7,200'. Lat. 9°32.92'N, long. 83°48.64'W. The turnoff from the PAH at kilometer 80 (at 9,400' elevation) descends for 5.5 kilometers into the valley of San Gerardo de Dota to Savegre Mountain Lodge (Albergue de Montaña Savegre, Cabinas Chacón) along the Río Savegre. This is an excellent area to see Black Guans, Resplendent Quetzals, Long-tailed Silky-Flycatchers, Black-faced Solitaires, Acorn Woodpeckers, Collared Trogons, and resident Red-tailed Hawks. Savegre Mountain Hotel, www.savegre.co.cr. Telephone: 506-2740-1028, 506-2740-1029; in USA (toll-free), 1-800-593-3305.

H-11: Transmission tower site, Cerro de la Muerte: Subalpine rain paramo. Elev. 10,800'. Lat. 9°33.25'N, long. 83°45.16'W. The gravel road leading to the transmission towers from the PAH is approximately at kilometer 90. It is an excellent place to

see Volcano Juncos, Peg-billed Finches, resident Red-tailed Hawks, and high-elevation wildflowers.

H-12: Vista del Valle: Elev. 5,650'. Lat. 9°27.78'N, long. 83°42.12 W. Vista del Valle is an excellent spot with both a restaurant and cabins (Cabins Mirador Vista del Valle) that provide birding along the PAH, at kilometer 119 as the highway begins its descent from Cerro de la Muerte to San Isidro del General. In late January and early February, this is an excellent location to watch Swallow-tailed Kites migrating north from South America. There are hummingbird feeders that feature the Violet Sabrewing, Red-headed Barbet, Cherrie's Tanager, Flame-colored Tanager, Bay-headed Tanager, and rare White-tailed Emerald. www.vistadelvallecr.com. Telephone: 506-2384-4685.

H-13: Bosque de Paz Ecolodge: Lower montane rainforest. Elev. 4,580'–8,000'. Lat. 10°12.272'N, 84°19.032'W. Bosque de Paz is an outstanding lodge on 1,800 acres of montane rainforest on the slope of Poás volcano. Birds of the area include the Resplendent

Quetzal, Golden-browed Chlorophonia, Long-tailed Silky-Flycatcher, Purple-throated Mountain-gem, Chestnut-capped Brush-Finch, and American Dipper. Black Guans come to the feeders in the courtyard by day, and tepescuintles, coatis, and agoutis come to the feeders in the evening. Address: P.O. Box 130-1000, San José, Costa Rica; www.bosquedepaz.com. Telephone: 506-2234-6676; e-mail: info@bosquedepaz.com.

H-14: Rincón de la Vieja NP: Premontane wet forest. Elev. 2,400'. Lat. 10°46.363'N, long. 85°20.002'W. This national park covers 34,992 acres, with a good system of trails and an interesting mix of wildlife characteristic of both rainforest and dry forest, including Great Curassows, Crested Guans, Long-tailed Manakins, woodcreepers, White-throated capuchin monkeys, and boa constrictors. There are also some unusual features like hot springs and bubbling mud pits. Telephone: Los Pailas administration office, 506-2661-8139; Guanacaste Conservation Area, 506-2666-5051; e-mail: acg@acguanacaste.ac.cr.

APPENDIX C: COSTA RICAN TRIP PREPARATION CHECKLIST

This trip preparation checklist has been prepared by Carrol and Ethelle Henderson and is based on their experience leading twenty-five birding tours to Costa Rica. The clothing and equipment listed are suggested for a two-week birding or natural history type of tour.

LUGGAGE

One or two pieces of soft, durable, canvas-type bags. Tagged and closed with small padlocks during air travel and storage at hotels. Think light! The less you bring, the easier your travel will be.

CLOTHING

Bring lightweight wash-and-wear clothes you can wash out yourself. Bring detergent double-bagged in self-sealing bags if laundry service is not available.

3–4 sets of field clothes: shirts/blouses; pants, shorts, or jeans; and one long-sleeved shirt.
Socks (4–5 pairs)
Underwear (4–5 pairs)
Handkerchiefs or tissues
Belt
Sweatshirt/sweater/light jacket
Towel (optional)
Hat or cap
Sleepwear
One pair walking shoes; one pair tennis or hiking shoes
Rain poncho or raincoat (lightweight)
Swimsuit and beach thongs
Wash cloth

TOILETRY ITEMS

Pack of Wet Ones or similar towelettes

Deodorant
Shaving cream
Toothbrush
Toothpaste/dental floss
Shampoo, without citronella base
Comb/hairbrush
Razor/shaver (electric current is 110 AC, but some outlets don't take wide prong; bring adapter plug)

PHOTO AND OPTIC EQUIPMENT

Camera with flash unit or video camera
Binoculars
Camera bag
Extra batteries for camera and flash unit and/or battery recharger
Lenses and filters
Lens tissue
Memory chips/film: 2 gigs/6 rolls--average interest in photos; 4 gigs/12 rolls—moderate interest; 8 gigs/24 rolls—enthusiastic. (Bring more than you think you will need. Film and memory chips can be hard to find and very expensive to buy on the road.)

OTHER EQUIPMENT

Fingernail clippers
Sunglasses
Suntan lotion or sunscreen (at least SPF 30)
Chapstick
Insect repellent (up to 30 percent DEET)
Aspirin
Imodium or Lomotil
Q-Tips
Notebook and pens
Small flashlight
Field guides
Knapsack/daypack/fannypack
Spending money, at least $400

in clean, undamaged bills (U.S. currency and credit cards are accepted in most hotels and larger stores. You can change some currency to Costa Rican colones at most hotels. Use colones in small towns.)
Prescriptions for personal medication, including original containers.
Travel alarm
Passport, plus photocopy packed separately from passport
Tip for naturalist guide (about $8–$12 per day)
Tip for driver (about $6–$8 per day)
Earplugs for sleeping near noisy highways or near loud surf
Umbrella (compact)

OTHER OPTIONAL ITEMS

Hunting or fishing vest for gear
Spare camera
Mending kit
Water bottle
20' cord for indoor clothesline

MAP

There is one exceptional map for Costa Rica that shows topographical features in great detail. Called a "tactical pilotage map," it is published by the U.S. Department of Defense. These maps are available for all regions of Latin America in a scale of 1:500,000. The map for Costa Rica is TPC K-25C. It can be ordered from the Latitudes Map and Travel Store in Minneapolis, Minnesota (www.latitudesmapstore.net), or from the NOAA Distribution Branch (N/CG33, National Ocean Service, Riverdale, MD 20737).

APPENDIX D: TRAVEL TIPS FOR A SUCCESSFUL WILDLIFE VIEWING TRIP IN COSTA RICA

1. Begin trip planning at least six months prior to your trip. The best lodges fill early during their high season from January to March. This is the dry season, which is typically the best time to visit Costa Rica. The first half of July can also be a good time to go.

2. Decide if you wish to travel independently or participate in a birding tour. A well-organized birding tour with a good guide and outfitter company will take care of logistics, driving, lodging arrangements, meals, and safety considerations. You will typically see two to four times more birds on a guided tour than if you travel by yourself.

3. Be aware that there are several levels of intensity for birding tour groups. Some groups are determined to see the maximum number of birds in the time available, around 400-plus species in two weeks. The pace is intense and is focused only on birds. Other birding groups are moderately paced. You may see about 300–350 bird species in two weeks with a group that is still focused primarily on birds

but takes time to enjoy a broader spectrum of the flora and fauna, like butterflies, flowers, and culture. General natural history groups are more passive, walk less, and are broadly interested in nature; you will see perhaps 100–125 species in two weeks. Get references and contact former clients to make sure you sign up for a group that matches your expectations, interests, and preferred level of physical activity.

4. Traveling by yourself can be cheaper, but you need to deal with lodging, meals, travel arrangements, and the Spanish language. If traveling by yourself, visit lodges that have naturalist birding guides, or lodges where you can hire local birding guides for day trips. Otherwise, hire a birding guide to accompany you on your entire trip.

5. When you finish eating at a restaurant, always check your tables and chair backs for binoculars, cameras, sunglasses, daypacks, and other items for yourself and for other members of your party.

6. While birding in Costa Rica, share the experience. After you have spotted a bird, help others in the group find it if they can't see it. If you encounter other birders or Costa Rican families while birding, let them take a peek through your spotting scope or binoculars if they have no optics.

7. When traveling in a bus, sit in a different seat every day to give everyone equal access to the best seats.

8. When birding along a narrow trail, switch positions with others every fifteen to twenty minutes to avoid dominating the best positions behind the guide.

9. When organizing your itinerary, try to include at least three of Costa Rica's biological zones (for example, Guanacaste, highlands, and Caribbean slope).

10. Bring any trip problems or complaints about your tour to the attention of your guide or tour leader in a discreet manner if you feel there is a problem in protocol, behavior, or group etiquette that needs to be addressed. Do not wait until after the trip to complain.

About the Author

Carrol L. Henderson, a native of Zearing, Iowa, received a bachelor of science degree in zoology from Iowa State University in 1968 and a master of forest resources degree in ecology from the University of Georgia in 1970. He did his graduate studies on the fish and wildlife of Costa Rica through the Organization for Tropical Studies and the University of Costa Rica.

Henderson joined the Minnesota Department of Natural Resources (DNR) in 1974 as assistant manager of the Lac qui Parle Wildlife Management Area near Milan. In 1977 he became supervisor of the DNR's newly created Nongame Wildlife Program, and he continues in that role to the present. During the past thirty-two years, Henderson developed a statewide program for the conservation of Minnesota's nongame wildlife and has planned and developed projects to help bring back bluebirds, Bald Eagles, Peregrine Falcons, River Otters, and Trumpeter Swans.

The author with his wife, Ethelle, in Costa Rica, 2005.

Henderson received the national Chevron Conservation Award in 1990, the 1992 Chuck Yeager Conservation Award from the National Fish and Wildlife Foundation, the 1993 Minnesota Award from the Minnesota Chapter of The Wildlife Society, and the 1994 Thomas Sadler Roberts Memorial Award from the Minnesota Ornithologists' Union.

His writings include *Woodworking for Wildlife, Landscaping for Wildlife, Wild about Birds: The DNR Bird Feeding Guide,* and co-authorship of *The Traveler's Guide to Wildlife in Minnesota* and *Lakescaping for Wildlife and Water Quality.* He also wrote the first edition of the *Field Guide to the Wildlife of Costa Rica* in 2002, *Oology and Ralph's Talking Eggs* in 2007, and *Birds in Flight: The Art and Science of How Birds Fly* in 2008. He is a regular contributor of feature stories in *Birder's World* and *Seasons* magazines.

An avid wildlife photographer, Henderson has taken most of the photos in his books and was the primary photographer for the 1995 book *Galápagos Islands: Wonders of the World.* His bird photography has been featured in the *New York Times, World Book Encyclopedia of Science, Audubon* magazine, and Discovery Online. He received seven national bird photography awards from *Wild Bird* magazine between 1995 and 1998.

Henderson and his wife, Ethelle, developed their expertise in tropical wildlife by leading forty-three birding tours to Latin America since 1987. This includes twenty-five trips to Costa Rica and additional trips to Panama, Belize, Nicaragua, Trinidad, Tobago, Venezuela, Bolivia, Chile, Ecuador, Brazil, Argentina, Peru, and the Galápagos Islands.

INDEX

Spanish names are set in **boldface text**.